Copyright © 2022 by Dragon Ryder

Cover Design by Dragon Ryder Publishing

ISBN 9798405111711

All rights reserved. No part of this book may be reproduced without written permission of the copyright owner, except for the use of limited quotations for the purpose of book reviews.

Owns This Book

MY GOALS

MY SCHEDULE

NOTE

WEEKLY PLAN

Saturday

Sunday

Munday

Tuesday

Thursday

Friday

Notes

WEEKLY PLAN

Saturday

Sunday

Munday

Tuesday

Thursday

Friday

Notes

WEEKLY PLAN

Saturday

Sunday

Munday

Tuesday

Thursday

Friday

Notes

WEEKLY PLAN

Saturday

Sunday

Munday

Tuesday

Thursday

Friday

Notes

WEEKLY PLAN

Saturday

Sunday

Munday

Tuesday

Thursday

Friday

Notes

SPOT THE DIFFERENCE
Spot the 5 differences below.

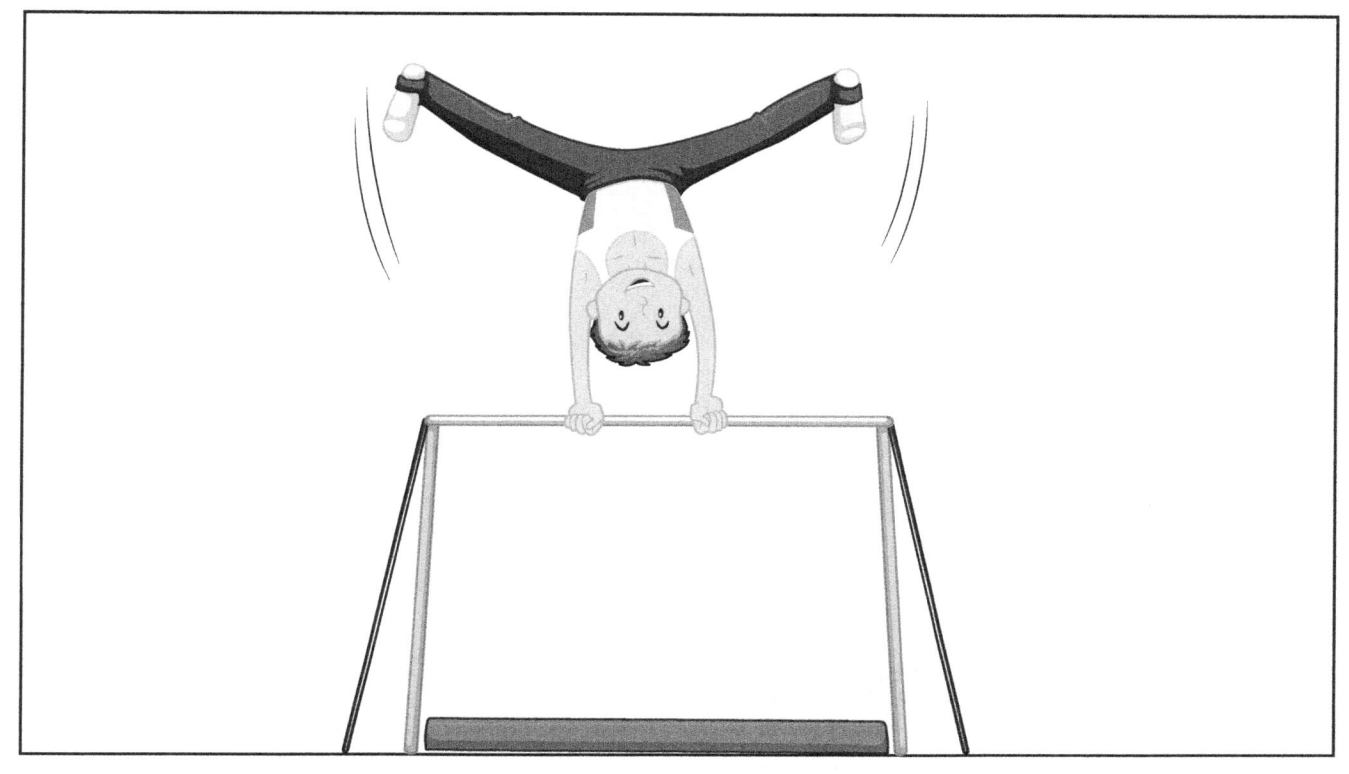

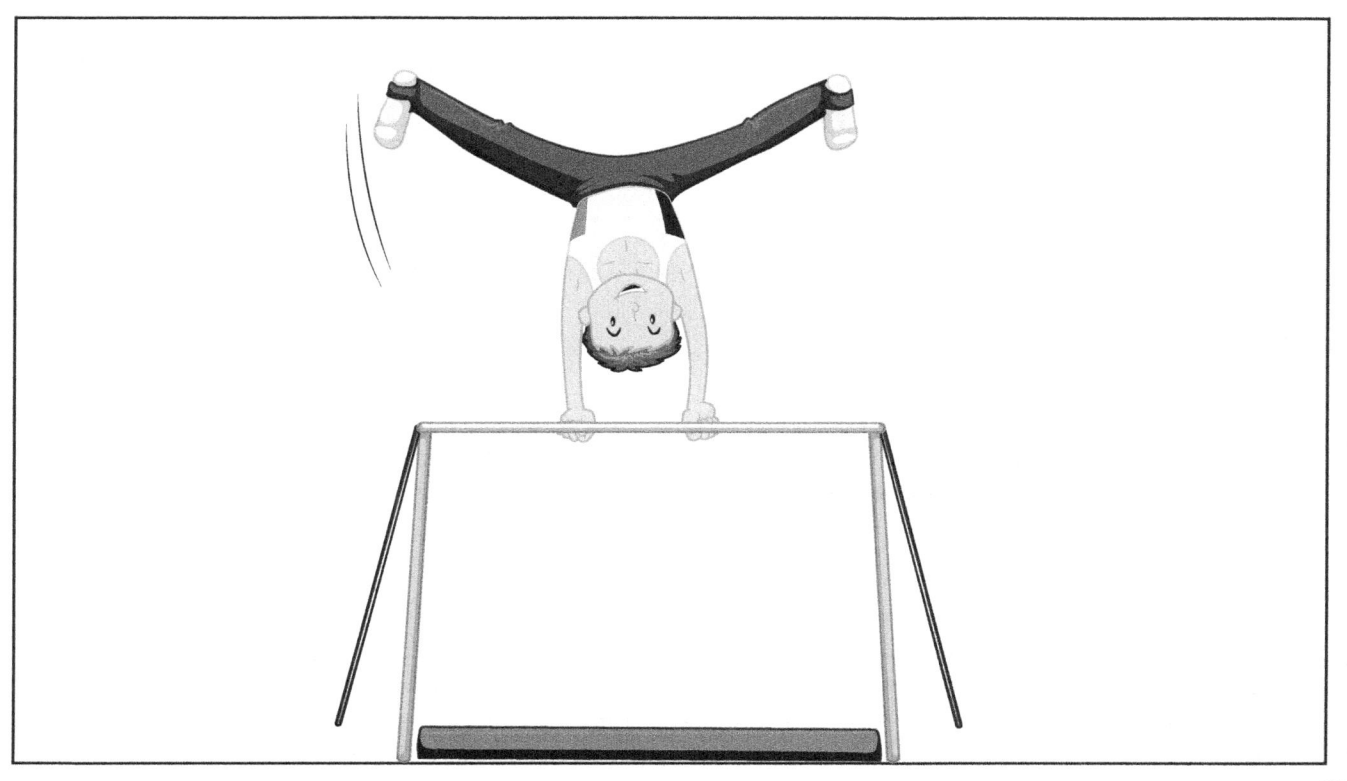

SPOT THE DIFFERENCE

Spot the 5 differences below.

SPOT THE DIFFERENCE
Spot the 5 differences below.

MY GOALS

MY SCHEDULE

NOTE

WEEKLY PLAN

Saturday

Sunday

Munday

Tuesday

Thursday

Friday

Notes

WEEKLY PLAN

Saturday

Sunday

Munday

Tuesday

Thursday

Friday

Notes

WEEKLY PLAN

Saturday

Sunday

Munday

Tuesday

Thursday

Friday

Notes

WEEKLY PLAN

Saturday

Sunday

Munday

Tuesday

Thursday

Friday

Notes

WEEKLY PLAN

Saturday	Sunday	Munday

Tuesday		Thursday

Friday	Notes

MAZE

Help the gymnast get to her ball so she could practice her Rhythmic gymnastic skills

4

MAZE

Can you find your way towards the right object required for this Rhythmic gymnastics?

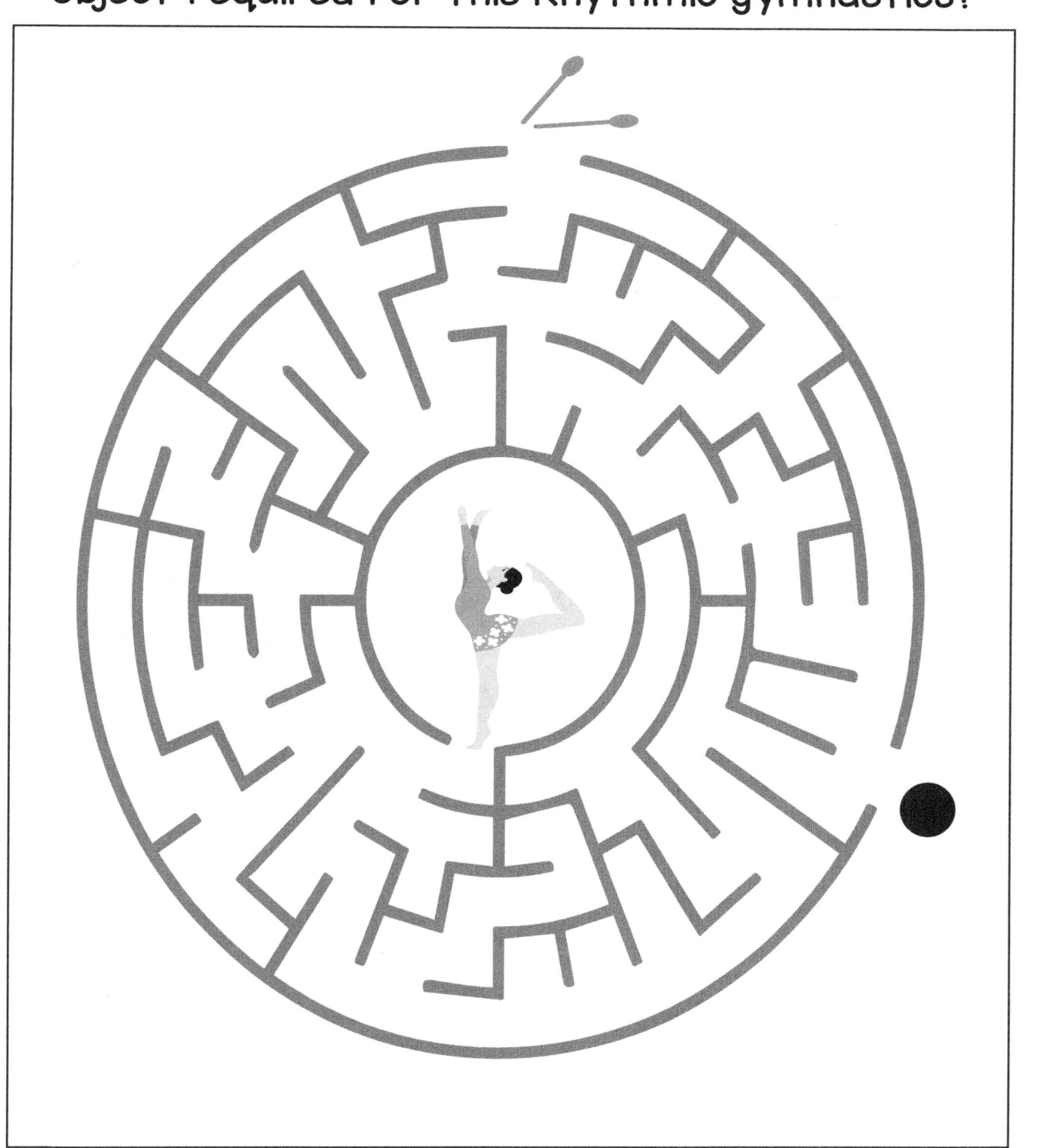

MAZE

Help the male gymnast find his female pair for them to practice their Aerobic gymnastics

6

MY GOALS

MY SCHEDULE

NOTE

WEEKLY PLAN

Saturday

Sunday

Munday

Tuesday

Thursday

Friday

Notes

WEEKLY PLAN

Saturday

Sunday

Munday

Tuesday

Thursday

Friday

Notes

WEEKLY PLAN

Saturday

Sunday

Munday

Tuesday

Thursday

Friday

Notes

WEEKLY PLAN

Saturday

Sunday

Munday

Tuesday

Thursday

Friday

Notes

WEEKLY PLAN

Saturday

Sunday

Munday

Tuesday

Thursday

Friday

Notes

COLORING

Color the picture below

COLORING

Color the picture below

8

MY GOALS

MY SCHEDULE

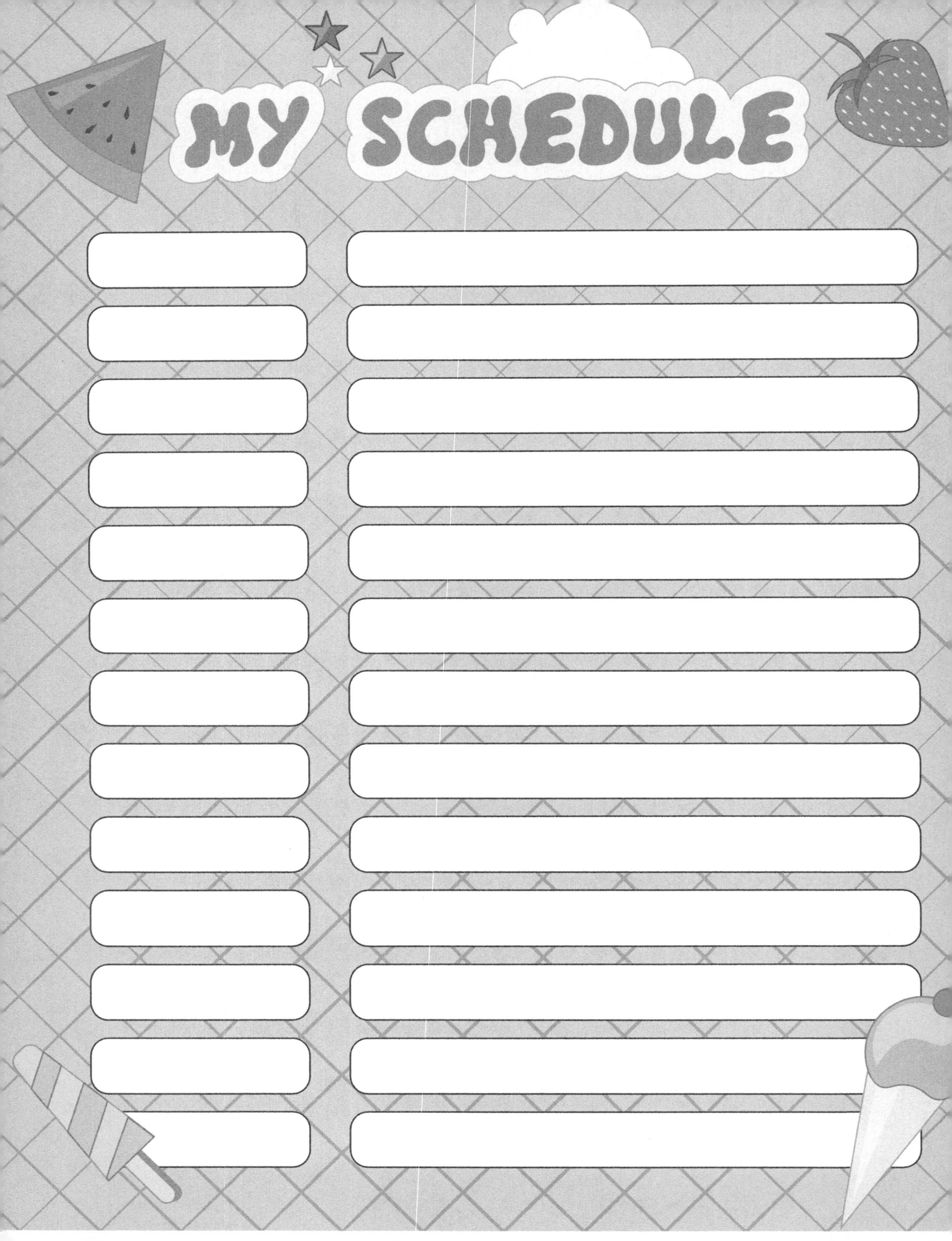

NOTE

WEEKLY PLAN

Saturday

Sunday

Munday

Tuesday

Thursday

Friday

Notes

WEEKLY PLAN

Saturday

Sunday

Munday

Tuesday

Thursday

Friday

Notes

WEEKLY PLAN

Saturday

Sunday

Munday

Tuesday

Thursday

Friday

Notes

WEEKLY PLAN

Saturday

Sunday

Munday

Tuesday

Thursday

Friday

Notes

WEEKLY PLAN

Saturday

Sunday

Munday

Tuesday

Thursday

Friday

Notes

COORDINATES

Help each gymnast find her coordinates.

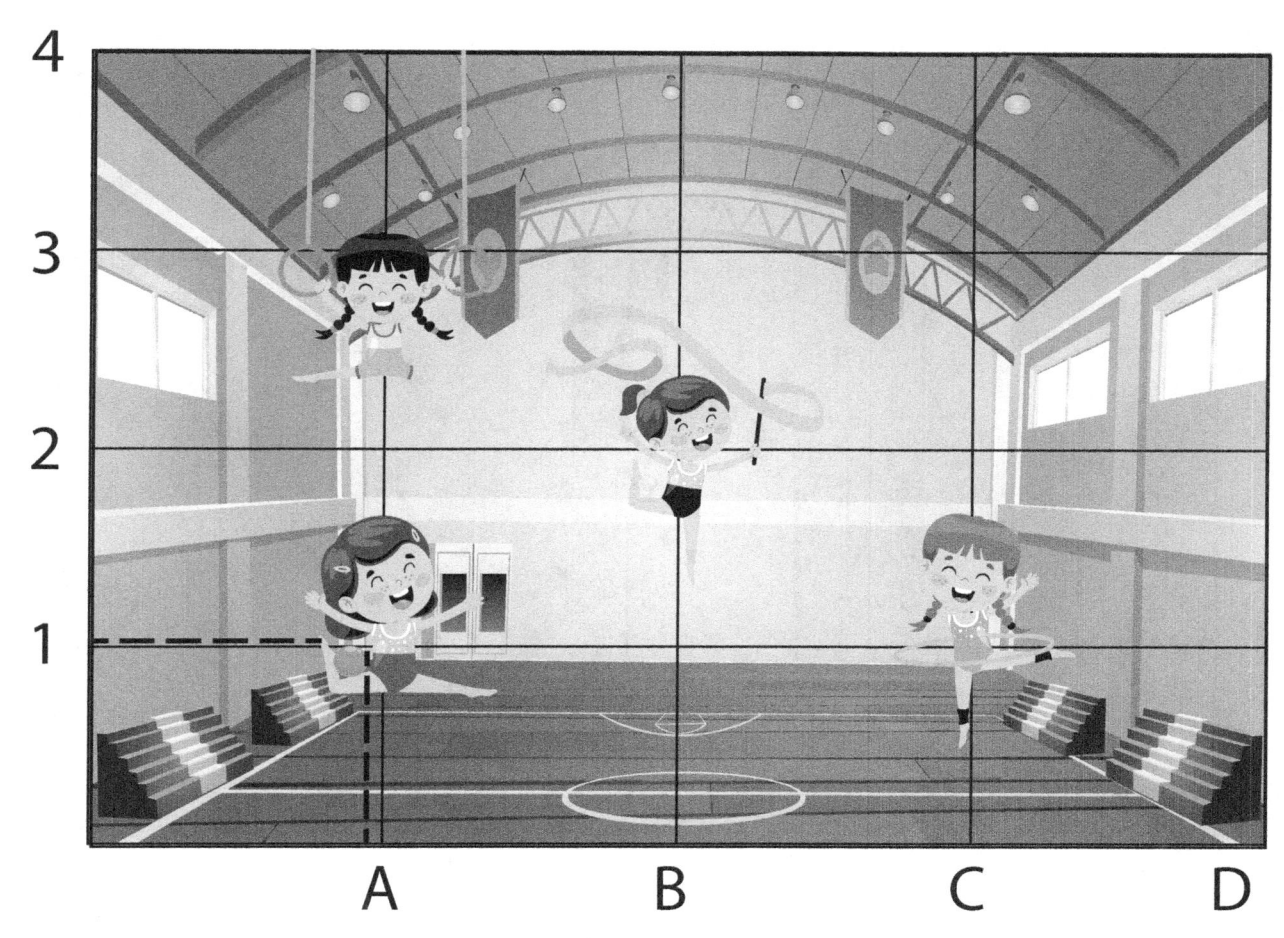

Follow the example to write the coordinates.

= (A , 1)

= (,   )

= (,   )

= (,   )

9

COORDINATES

Can you locate the coordinates of each object?

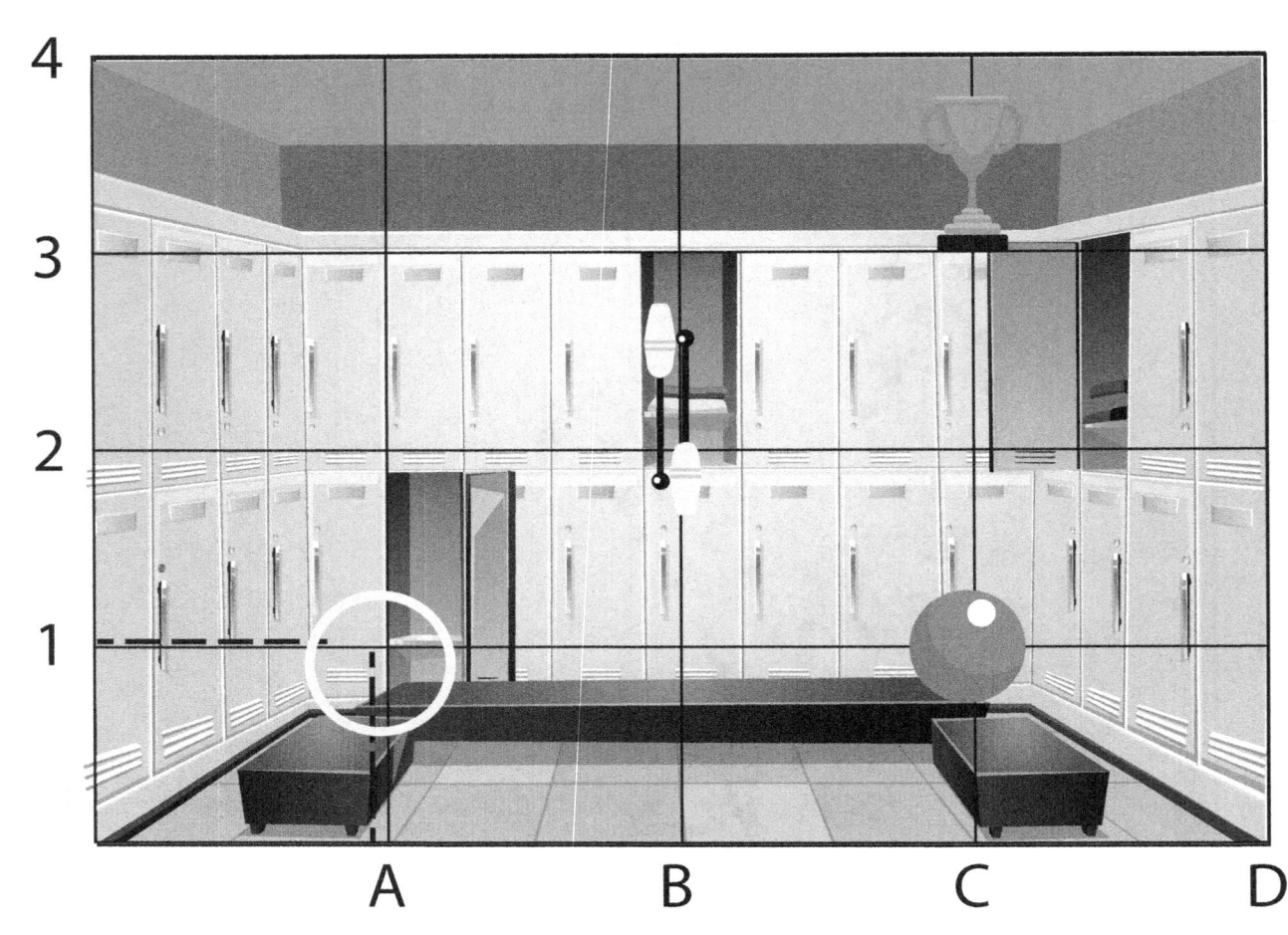

Follow the example to write the coordinates.

◯ = (A , 1)

🏆 = (,)

= (,)

⚪ = (,)

MY GOALS

MY SCHEDULE

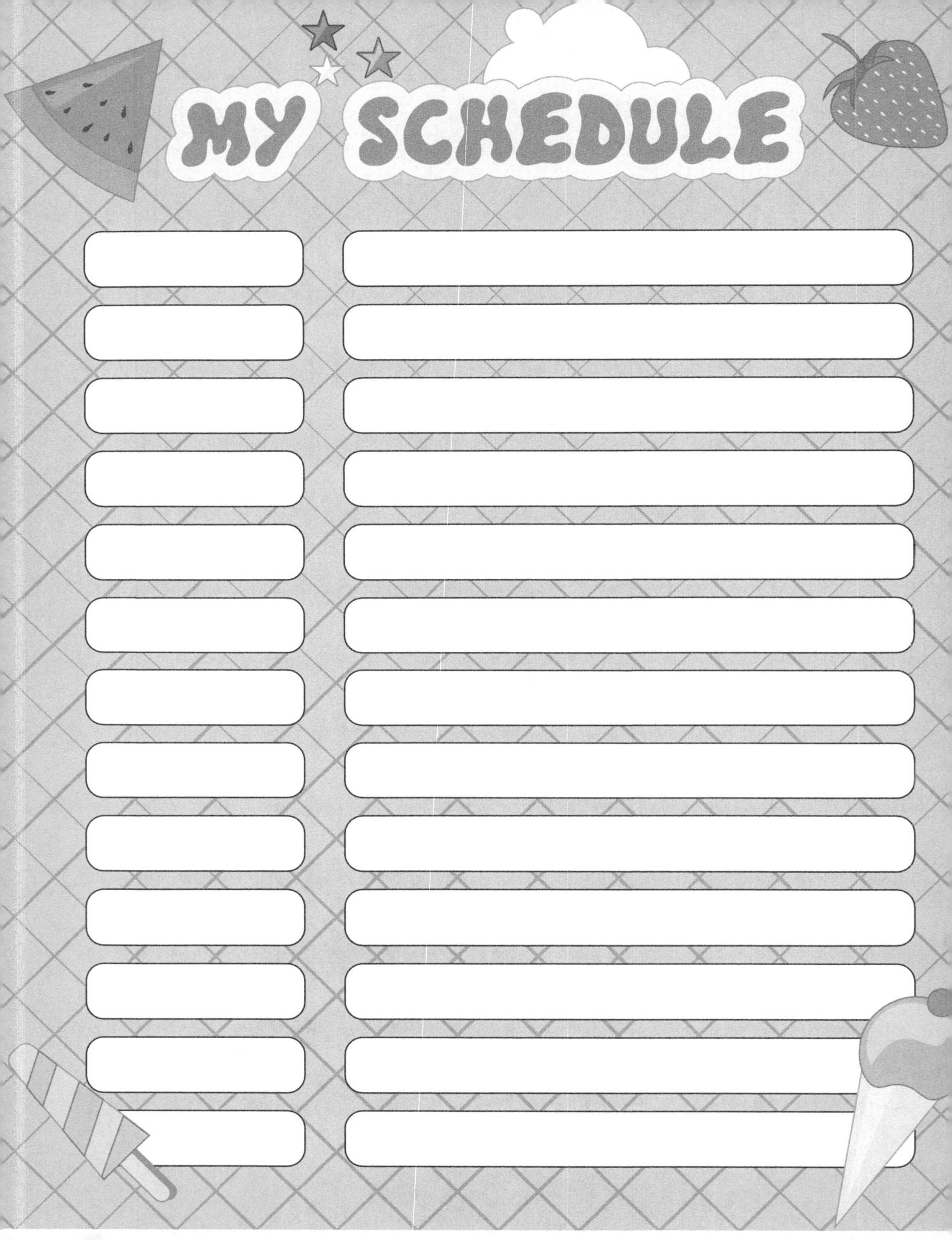

NOTE

WEEKLY PLAN

Saturday

Sunday

Munday

Tuesday

Thursday

Friday

Notes

WEEKLY PLAN

Saturday

Sunday

Munday

Tuesday

Thursday

Friday

Notes

WEEKLY PLAN

Saturday

Sunday

Munday

Tuesday

Thursday

Friday

Notes

WEEKLY PLAN

Saturday

Sunday

Munday

Tuesday

Thursday

Friday

Notes

WEEKLY PLAN

Saturday

Sunday

Munday

Tuesday

Thursday

Friday

Notes

MATH MAZE

Can you help Gina cross all 16 numbers and get to the 1st position?

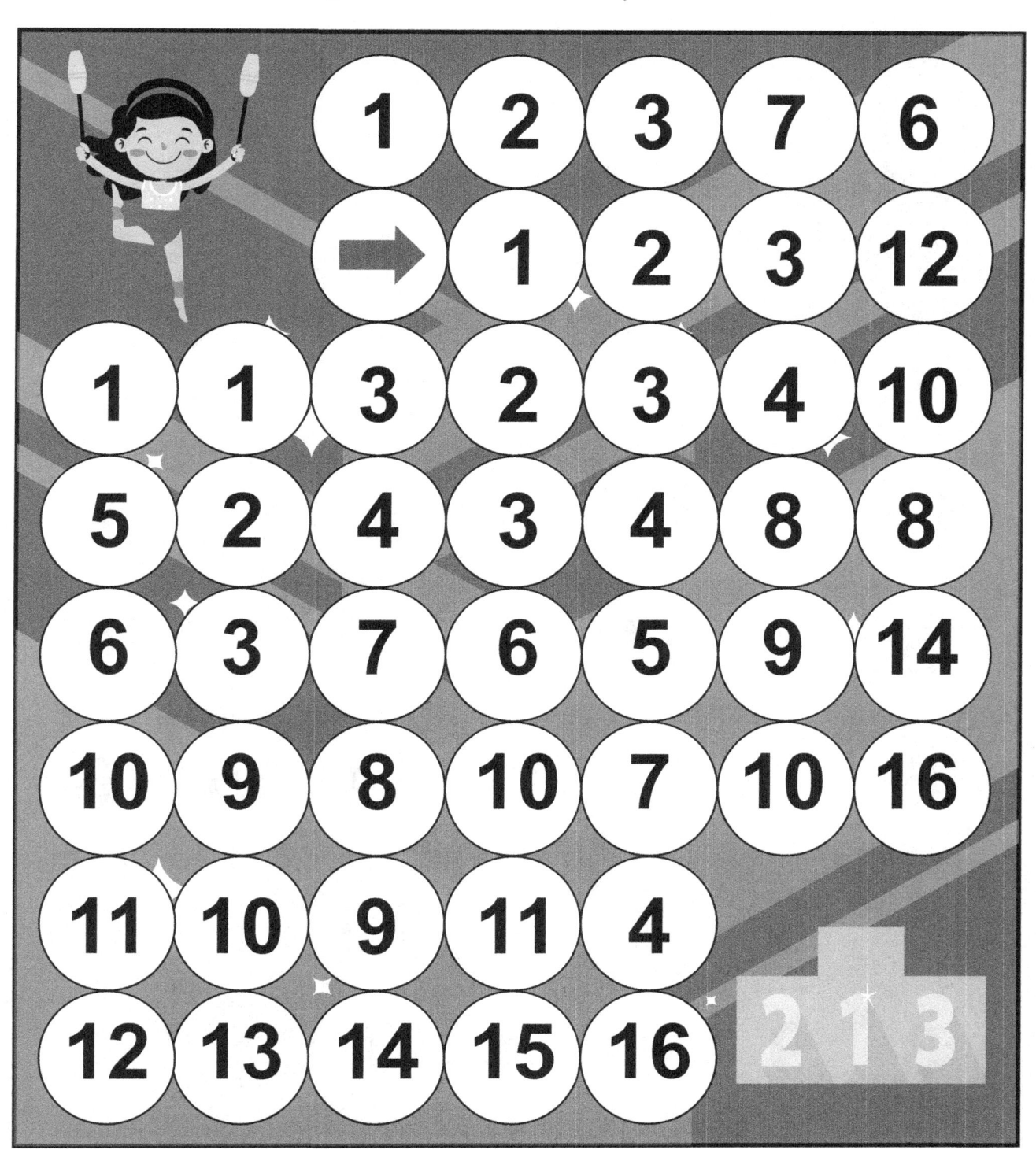

	1	2	3	7	6
→	1	2	3	12
1	1	3	2	3	4	10
5	2	4	3	4	8	8
6	3	7	6	5	9	14
10	9	8	10	7	10	16
11	10	9	11	4		
12	13	14	15	16	2 1 3

11

MATH MAZE

Cross all the 16 numbers to match the pair of clubs with each other.

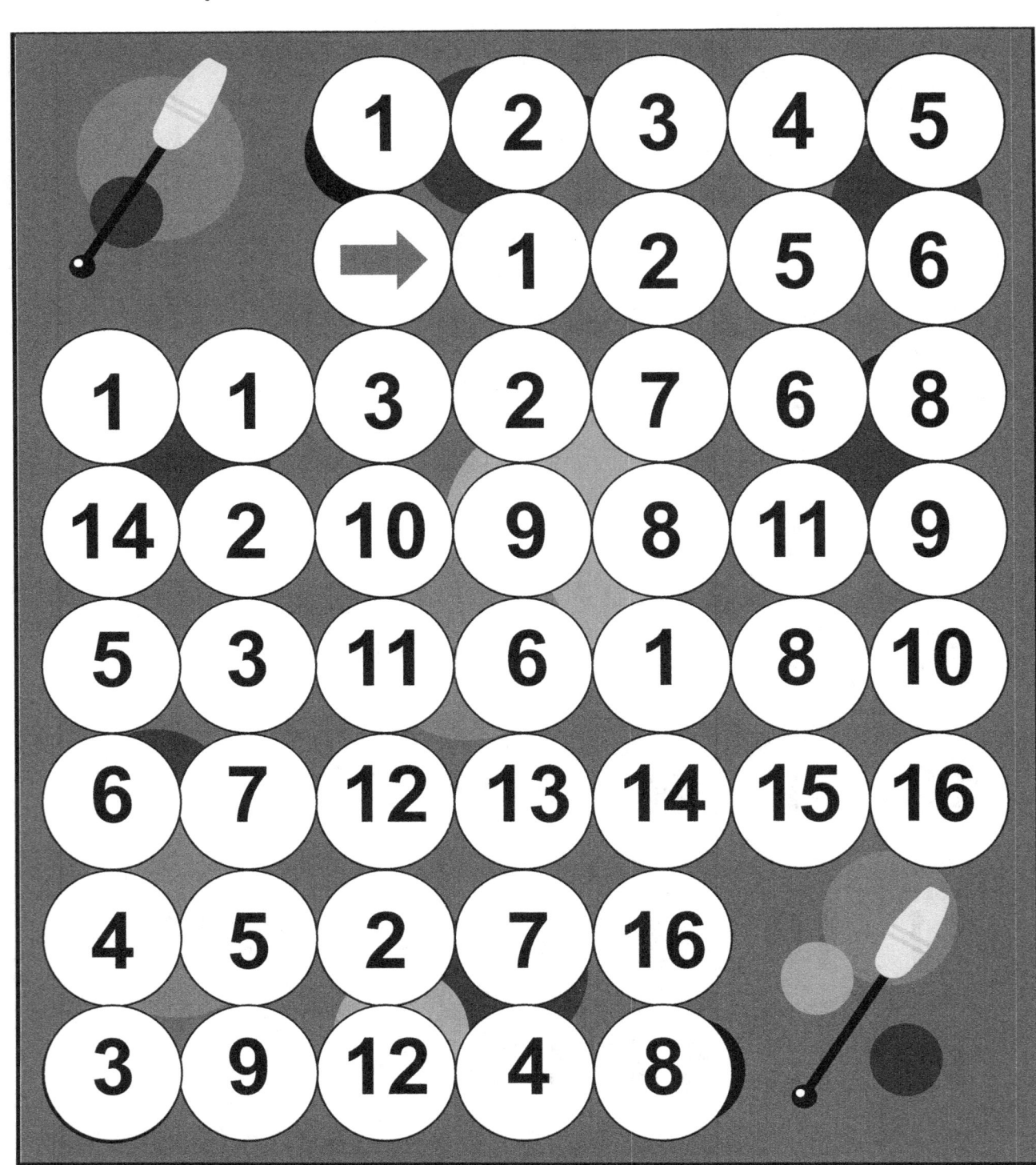

	1	2	3	4	5
	→	1	2	5	6
1	1	3	2	7	6	8
14	2	10	9	8	11	9
5	3	11	6	1	8	10
6	7	12	13	14	15	16
	4	5	2	7	16
	3	9	12	4	8

12

MY GOALS

MY SCHEDULE

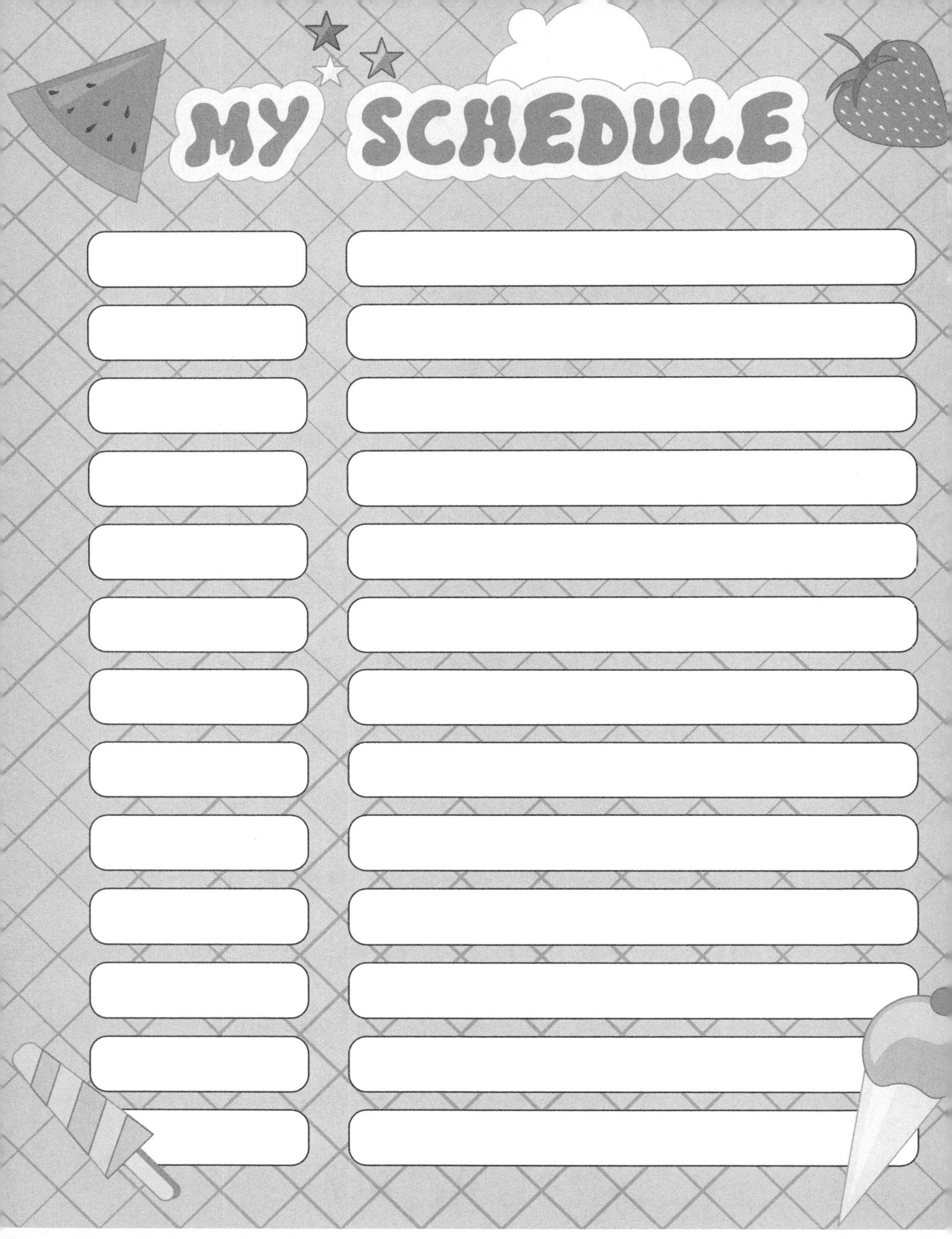

NOTE

WEEKLY PLAN

Saturday

Sunday

Munday

Tuesday

Thursday

Friday

Notes

WEEKLY PLAN

Saturday

Sunday

Munday

Tuesday

Thursday

Friday

Notes

WEEKLY PLAN

Saturday

Sunday

Munday

Tuesday

Thursday

Friday

Notes

WEEKLY PLAN

| Saturday | Sunday | Munday |

| Tuesday | | Thursday |

| Friday | Notes |

WEEKLY PLAN

Saturday

Sunday

Munday

Tuesday

Thursday

Friday

Notes

ODD ONE OUT

Can you find the odd outfit from each list and circle it?

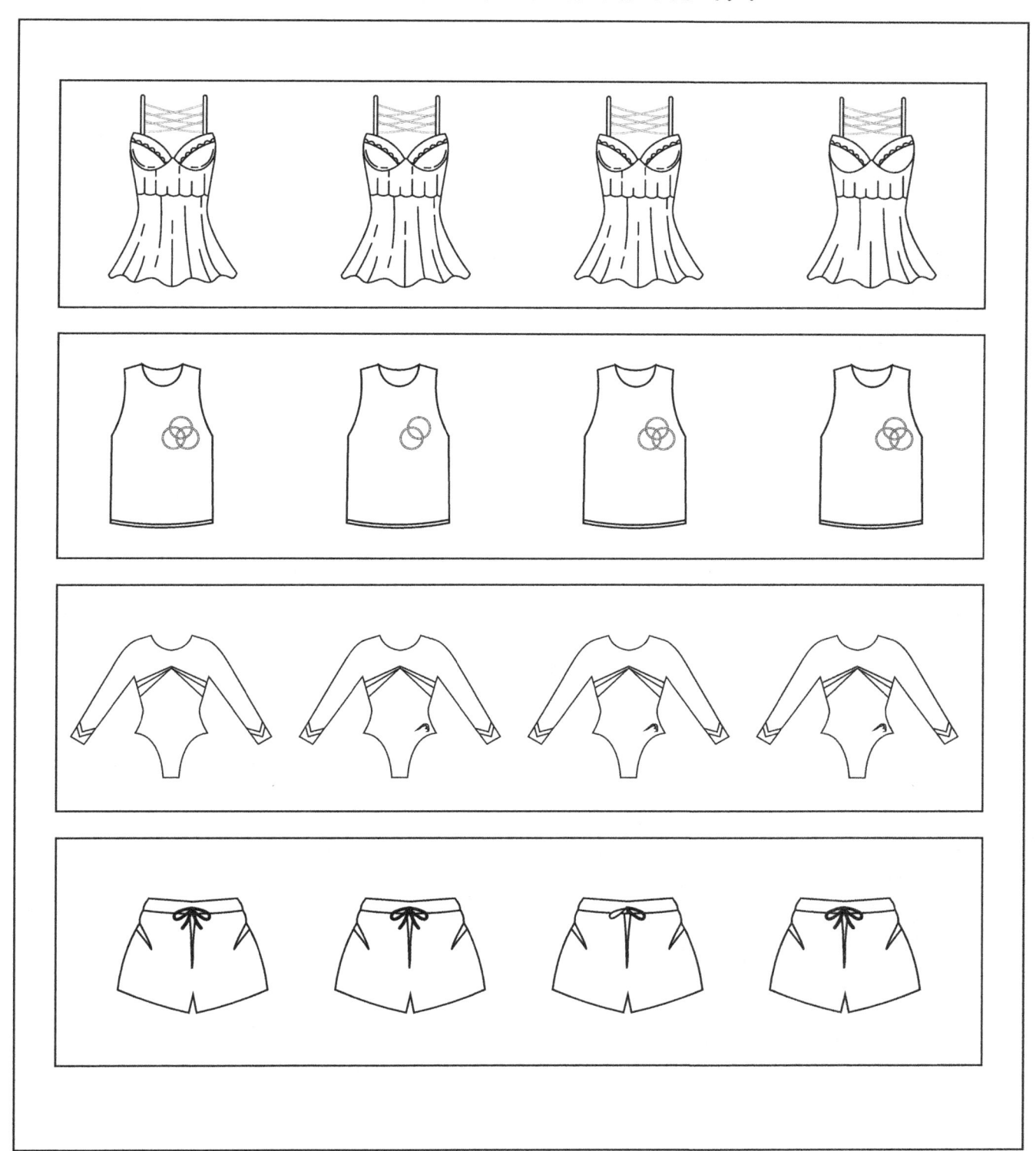

13

ODD ONE OUT

Can you find the odd hoop from each list and tick it?

MY GOALS

MY SCHEDULE

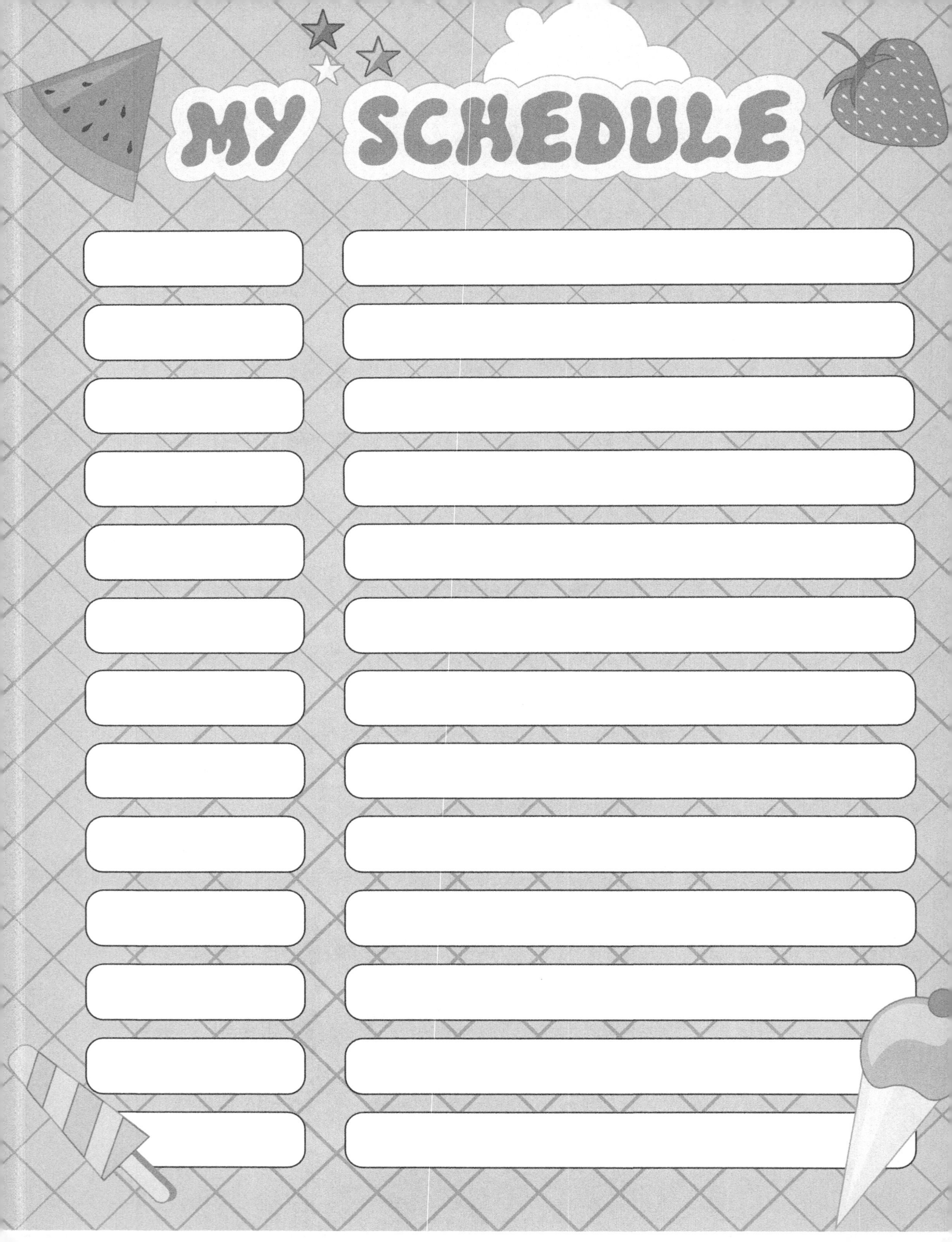

NOTE

WEEKLY PLAN

Saturday

Sunday

Munday

Tuesday

Thursday

Friday

Notes

WEEKLY PLAN

Saturday

Sunday

Munday

Tuesday

Thursday

Friday

Notes

WEEKLY PLAN

Saturday

Sunday

Munday

Tuesday

Thursday

Friday

Notes

WEEKLY PLAN

Saturday

Sunday

Munday

Tuesday

Thursday

Friday

Notes

WEEKLY PLAN

Saturday

Sunday

Munday

Tuesday

Thursday

Friday

Notes

DOT TO DOT

Trace all 1-20 dots to complete the picture

15

DOT TO DOT

Trace all 1-35 dots to complete the picture

16

MY GOALS

MY SCHEDULE

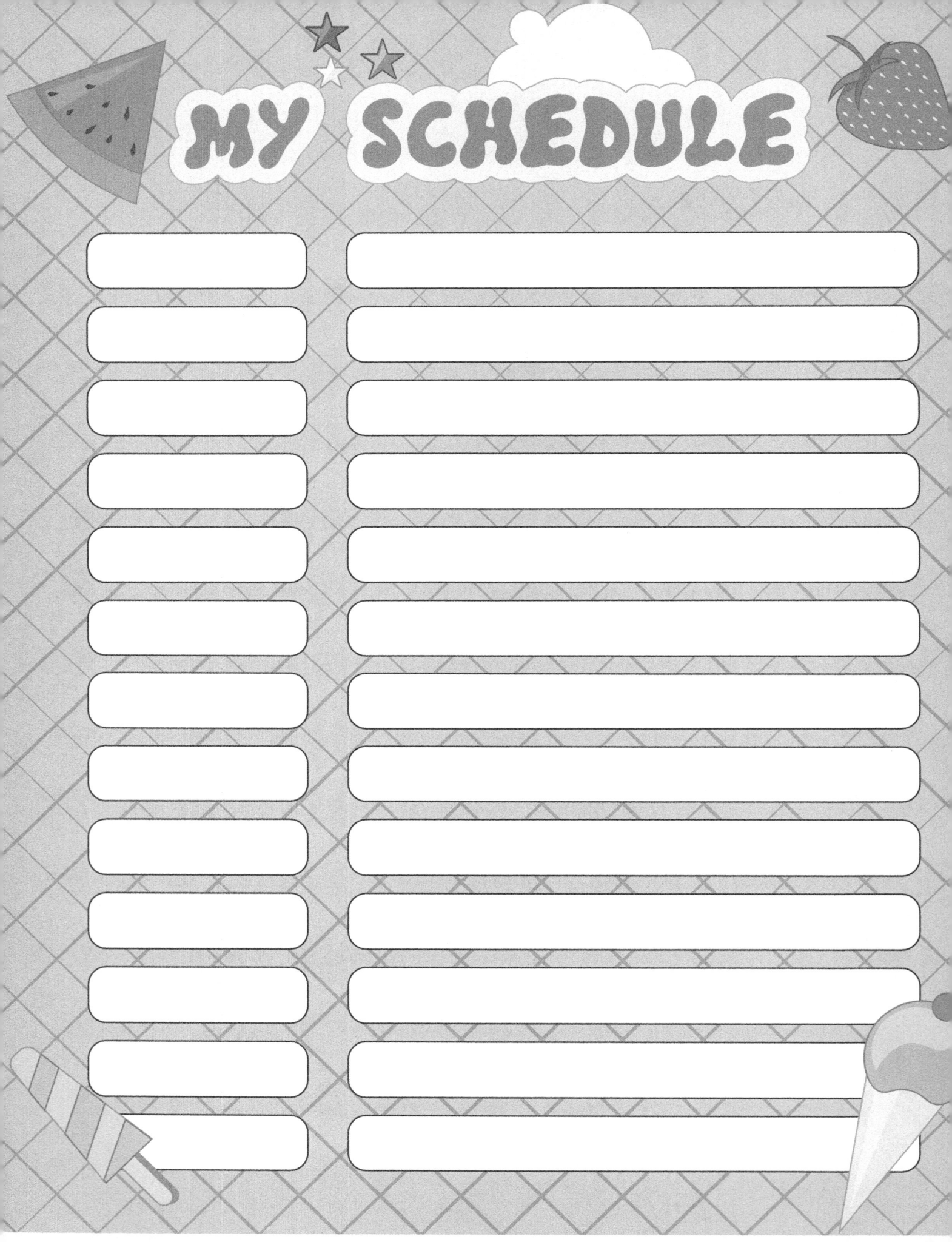

NOTE

WEEKLY PLAN

Saturday

Sunday

Munday

Tuesday

Thursday

Friday

Notes

WEEKLY PLAN

Saturday

Sunday

Munday

Tuesday

Thursday

Friday

Notes

WEEKLY PLAN

Saturday

Sunday

Munday

Tuesday

Thursday

Friday

Notes

WEEKLY PLAN

Saturday

Sunday

Munday

Tuesday

Thursday

Friday

Notes

WEEKLY PLAN

Saturday

Sunday

Munday

Tuesday

Thursday

Friday

Notes

FINISH THE PATTERN
Tick the correct order of the pattern

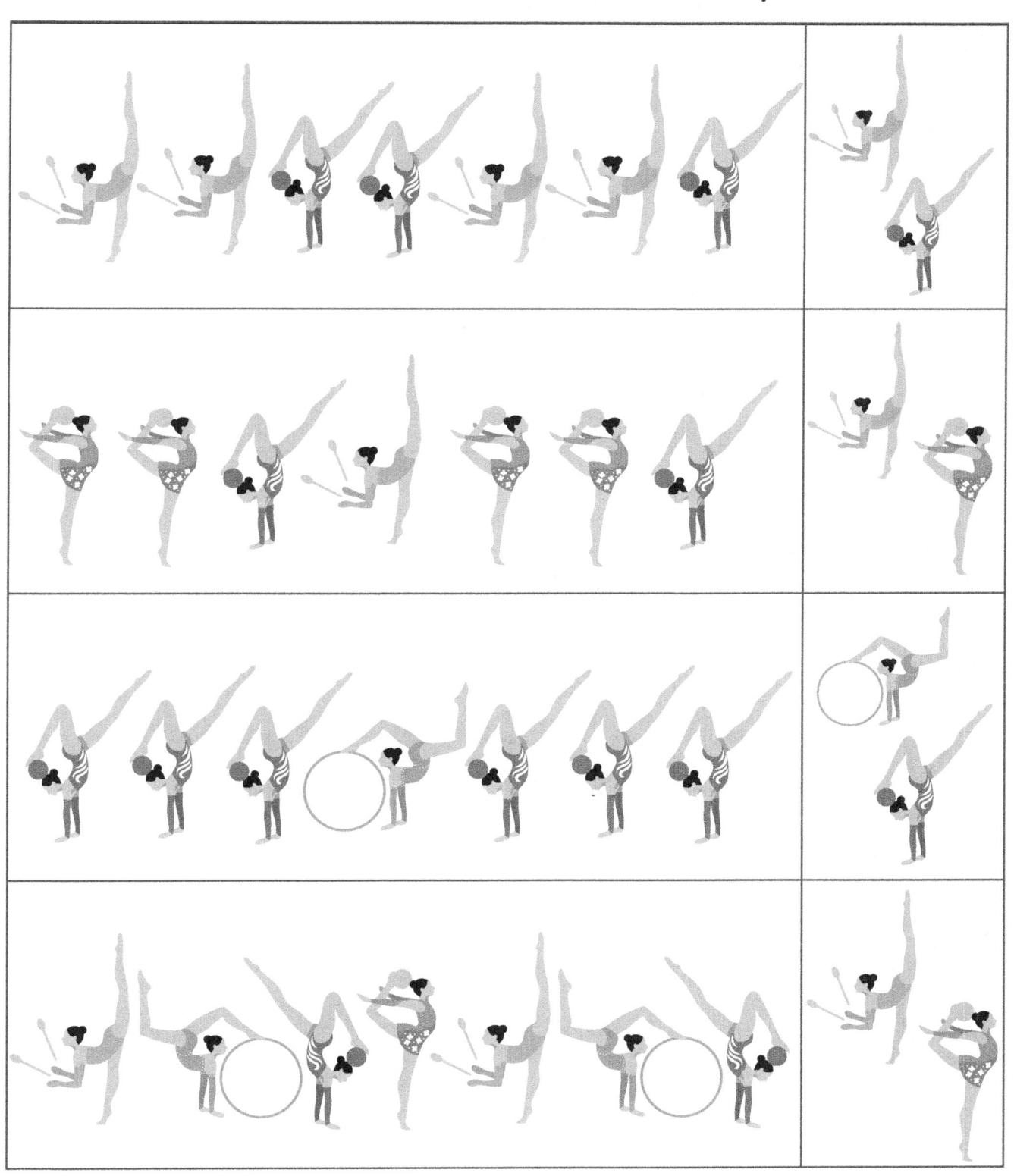

FINISH THE PATTERN

Paste the correct order of the pattern

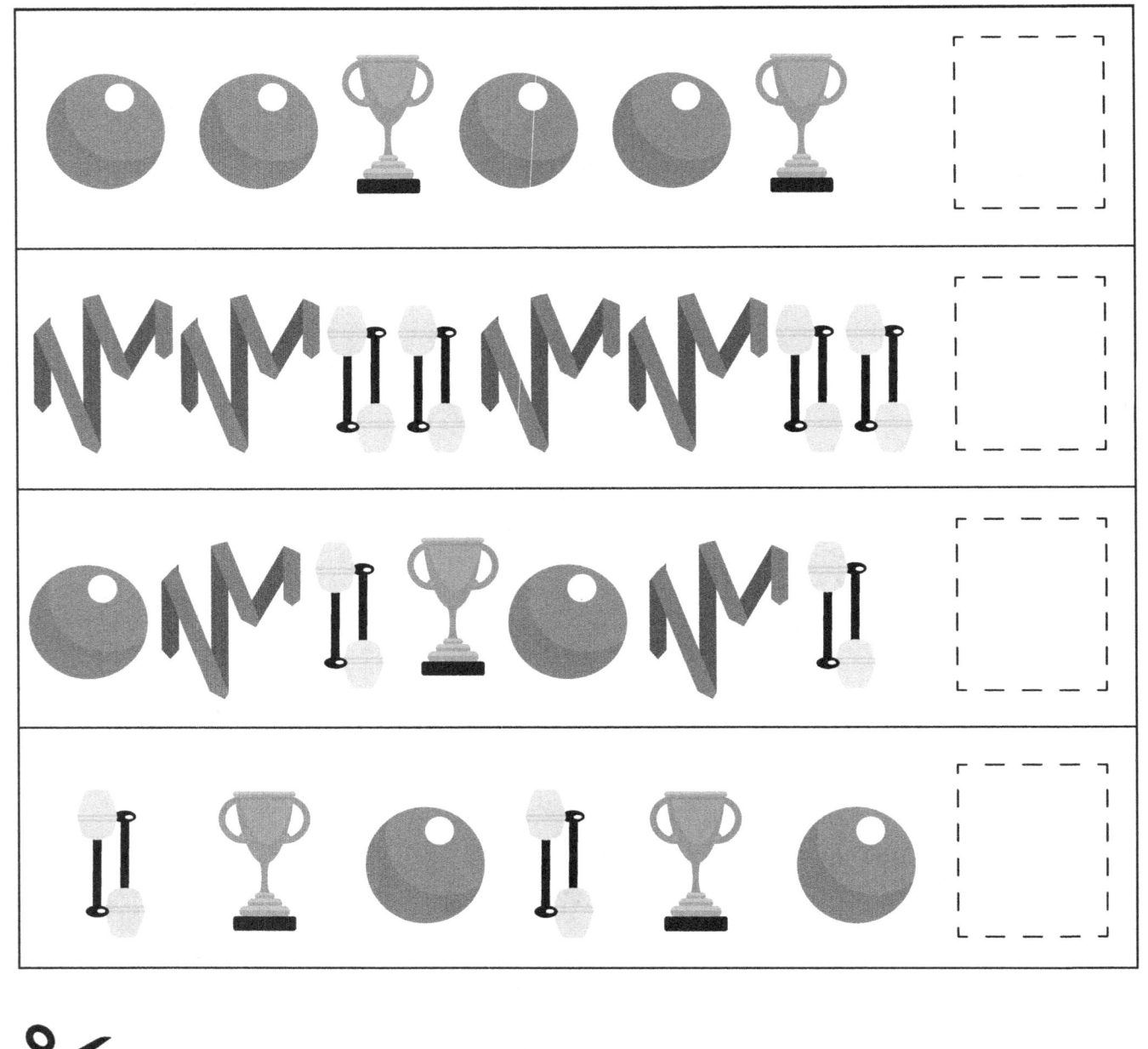

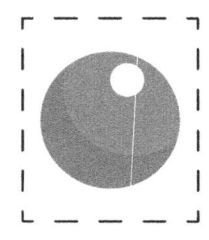

MY GOALS

MY SCHEDULE

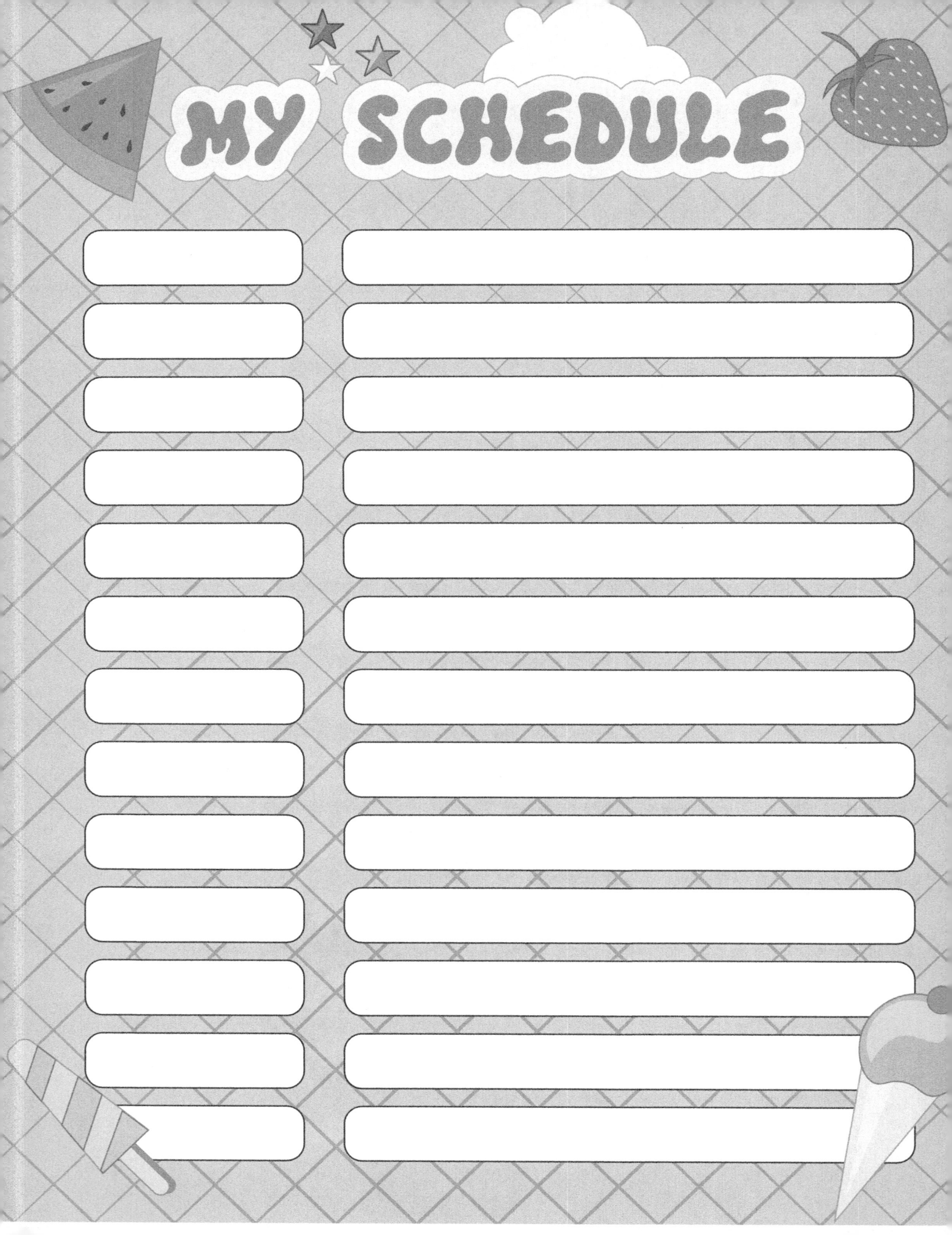

NOTE

WEEKLY PLAN

Saturday

Sunday

Munday

Tuesday

Thursday

Friday

Notes

WEEKLY PLAN

Saturday

Sunday

Munday

Tuesday

Thursday

Friday

Notes

WEEKLY PLAN

Saturday

Sunday

Munday

Tuesday

Thursday

Friday

Notes

WEEKLY PLAN

Saturday

Sunday

Munday

Tuesday

Thursday

Friday

Notes

WEEKLY PLAN

Saturday

Sunday

Munday

Tuesday

Thursday

Friday

Notes

WORD SEARCH

Search all the words given below

P	O	M	M	E	L	H	O	R	S	E	T
B	A	V	U	R	H	Y	S	D	K	J	F
E	E	J	T	U	M	B	L	I	N	G	G
A	B	J	R	E	A	T	V	S	T	B	Y
M	A	M	A	P	T	L	U	R	A	E	M
S	D	U	M	L	S	S	P	H	F	K	N
Q	I	A	P	Q	A	G	M	Y	J	H	A
U	B	F	O	V	A	U	L	T	O	M	S
G	A	K	L	J	C	T	E	H	Z	Y	T
B	R	G	I	G	I	A	K	M	D	H	I
T	N	R	N	D	L	E	Z	I	J	Z	C
F	C	A	E	R	O	B	I	C	Q	B	S

Find the hidden words in these directions ➡ ⬇

GYMNASTICS	BARS	POMMEL HORSE
AEROBIC	BEAMS	MATS
RHYTHMIC	TUMBLING	
VAULT	TRAMPOLINE	

20

CROSSWORD PUZZLE

Search all the words given below

Down ⬇

SQUAT
SWING
BARRIER
HOOP
FLOOR

Across ➡

TRAMPOLINE
RINGS
CARTWHEEL

25

MY GOALS

MY SCHEDULE

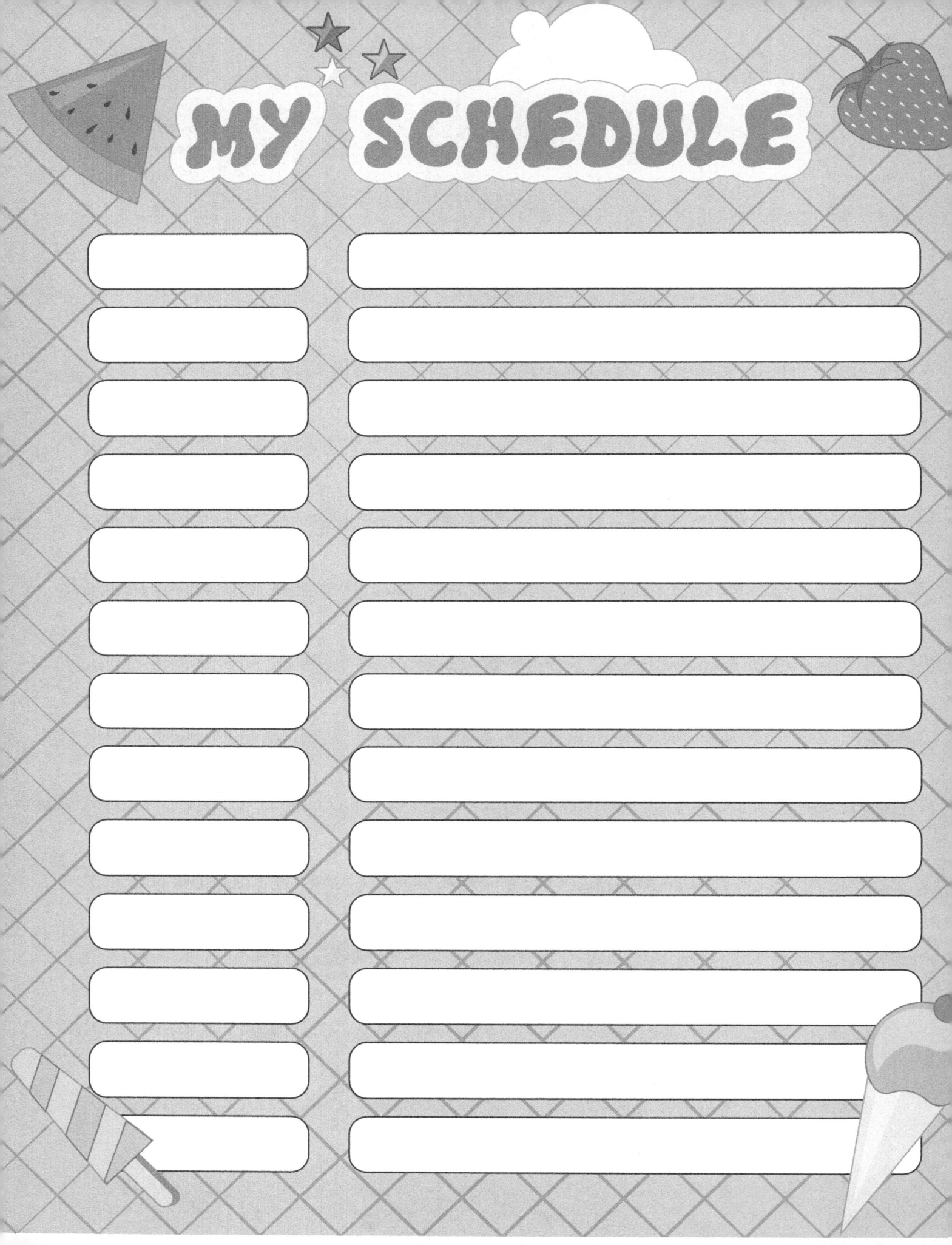

NOTE

WEEKLY PLAN

Saturday

Sunday

Munday

Tuesday

Thursday

Friday

Notes

WEEKLY PLAN

Saturday

Sunday

Munday

Tuesday

Thursday

Friday

Notes

WEEKLY PLAN

Saturday

Sunday

Munday

Tuesday

Thursday

Friday

Notes

WEEKLY PLAN

Saturday

Sunday

Munday

Tuesday

Thursday

Friday

Notes

WEEKLY PLAN

Saturday

Sunday

Munday

Tuesday

Thursday

Friday

Notes

ADDITION

Add the numbers together to find the sum

☐ + ☐ = ☐

☐ + ☐ = ☐

☐ + ☐ = ☐

☐ + ☐ = ☐

☐ + ☐ = ☐

ADDITION

Join the correct sums.

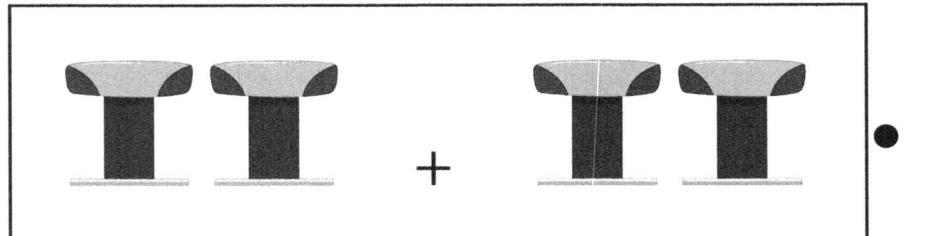

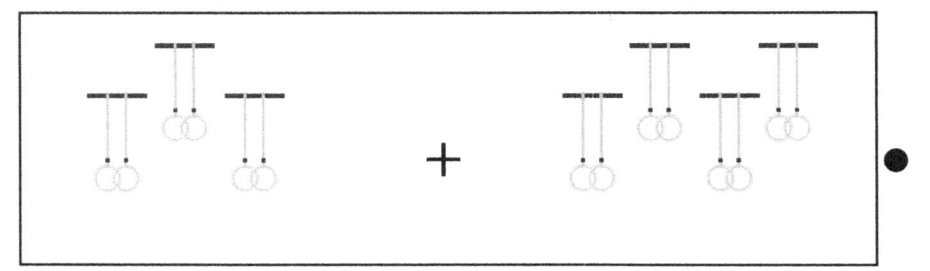

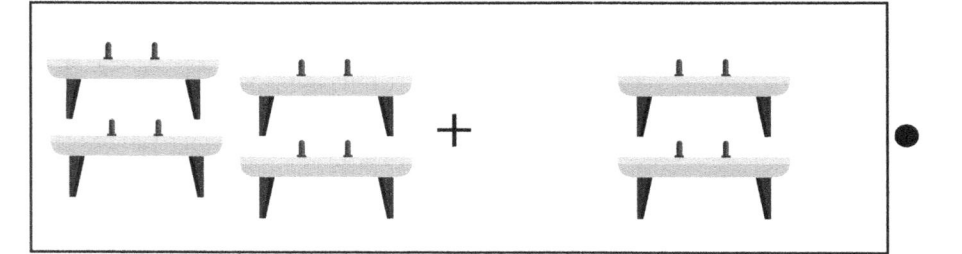

- 7
- 10
- 4
- 6 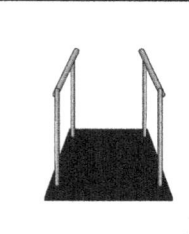 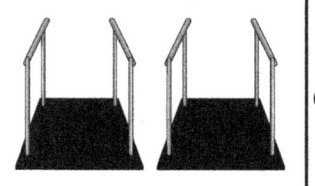
- 3

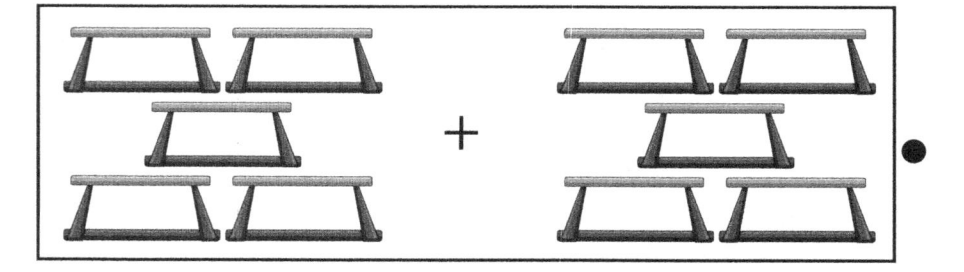

SUBTRACTION

Subtract the numbers to get the answer.

SUBTRACTION

Join the correct subtraction.

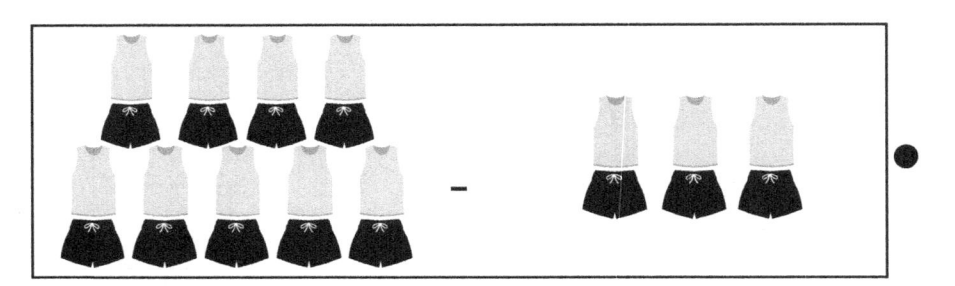

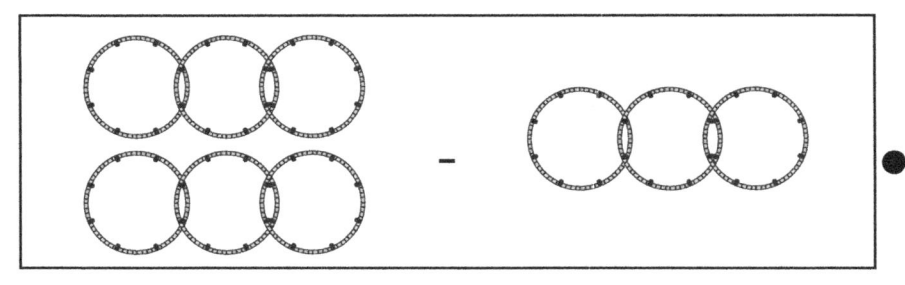

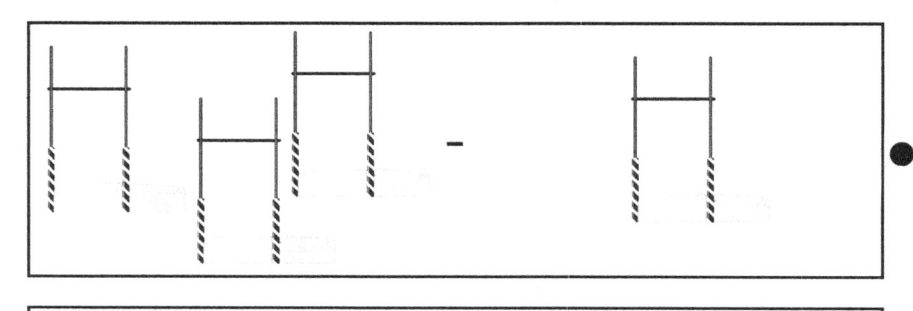

- 3
- 4
- 6 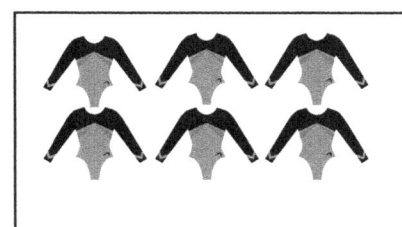 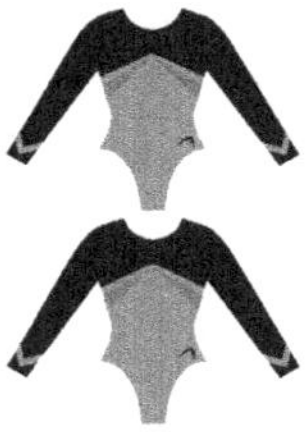
- 7
- 2

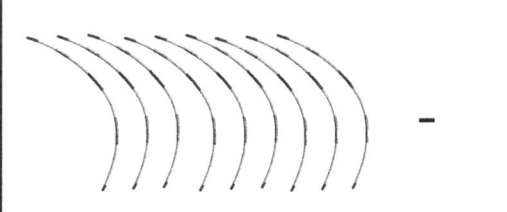

MY GOALS

MY SCHEDULE

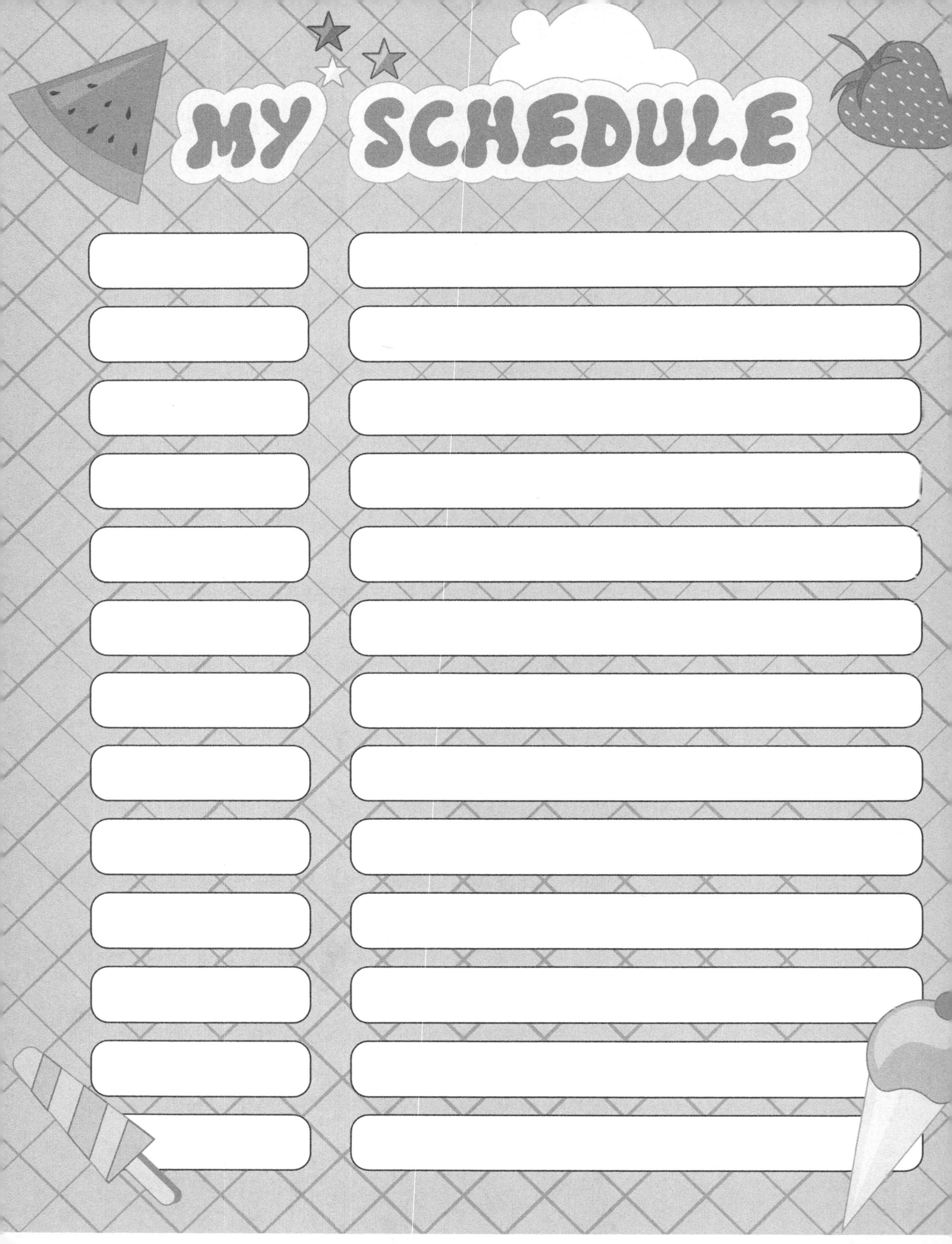

NOTE

WEEKLY PLAN

Saturday

Sunday

Munday

Tuesday

Thursday

Friday

Notes

WEEKLY PLAN

Saturday

Sunday

Munday

Tuesday

Thursday

Friday

Notes

WEEKLY PLAN

Saturday

Sunday

Munday

Tuesday

Thursday

Friday

Notes

WEEKLY PLAN

Saturday

Sunday

Munday

Tuesday

Thursday

Friday

Notes

WEEKLY PLAN

Saturday

Sunday

Munday

Tuesday

Thursday

Friday

Notes

CRACK THE CODE

Solve the addition and subtraction problems and fill the lines with letters at the bottom from matching the answers.

7 - 1 = ____ (a)   2 - 1 = ____ (h)

8 + 1 = ____ (s)   5 + 2 = ____ (f)

6 - 4 = ____ (p)   14 - 3 = ____ (a)

2 + 3 = ____ (i)   8 + 6 = ____ (e)

10 + 3 = ____ (l)   12 - 9 = ____ (d)

Crack the code from the answers above.

What did the gymnast do when she got angry?

___ ___ ___   ___ ___ ___ ___ ___ ___ ___
 9   1   14   7   13   5   2   2   14   3

WORD SCRAMBLE

Rewrite the correct order of the scrambled words below

lempom heros

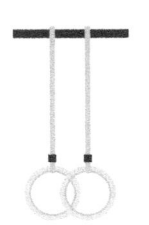

_____

litls nirsg

_____

sedalm

_____

taulv

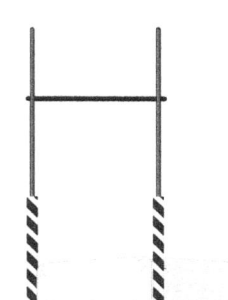

_____

gihh arb

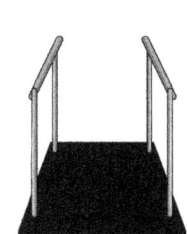

_____

lelpalra sarb

_____

30

MY GOALS

MY SCHEDULE

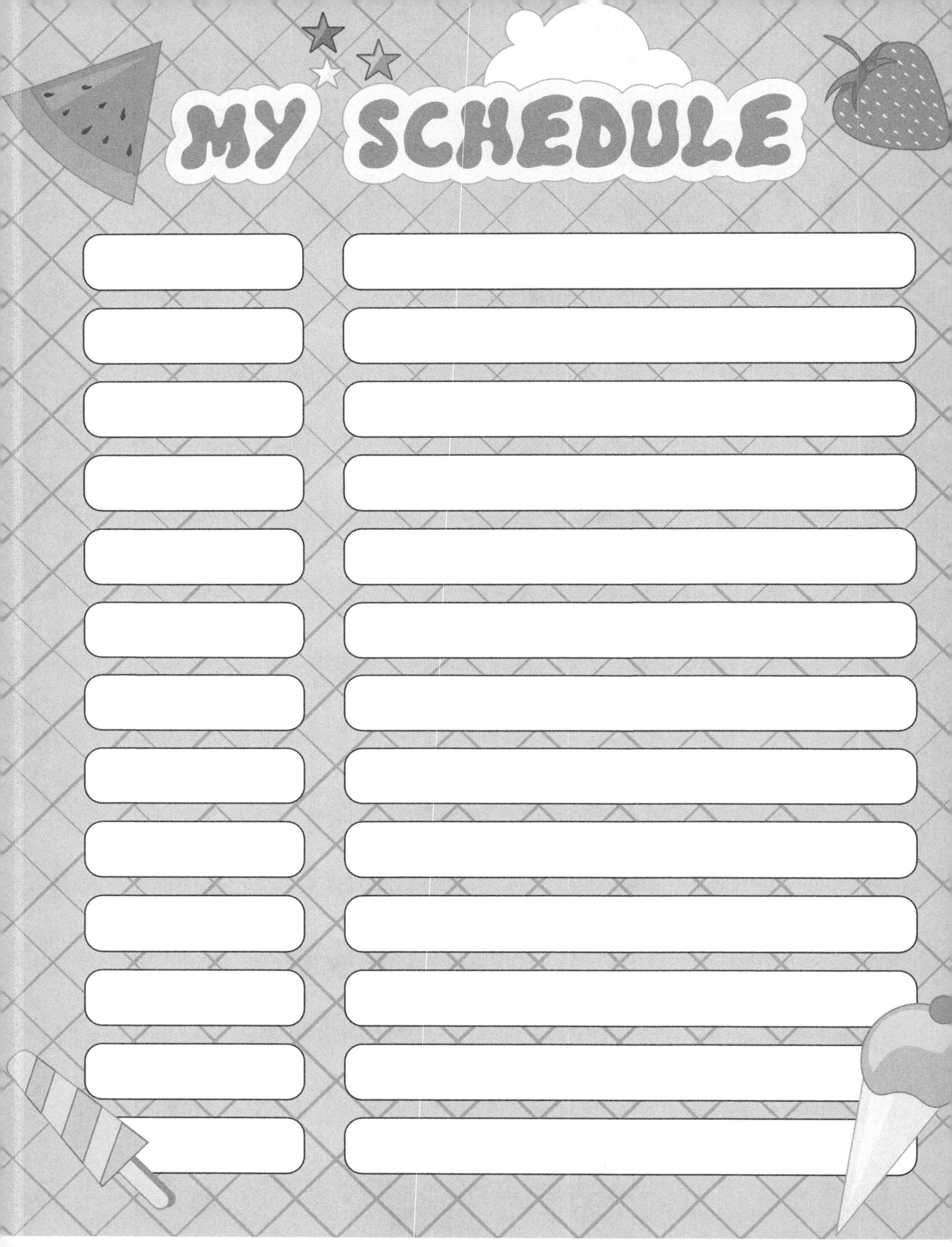

NOTE

WEEKLY PLAN

Saturday

Sunday

Munday

Tuesday

Thursday

Friday

Notes

WEEKLY PLAN

Saturday

Sunday

Munday

Tuesday

Thursday

Friday

Notes

WEEKLY PLAN

| Saturday | Sunday | Munday |

| Tuesday | | Thursday |

| Friday | Notes |

WEEKLY PLAN

Saturday

Sunday

Munday

Tuesday

Thursday

Friday

Notes

WEEKLY PLAN

Saturday

Sunday

Munday

Tuesday

Thursday

Friday

Notes

IDENTIFY THE SHADOW

Match the correct shadow of the picture

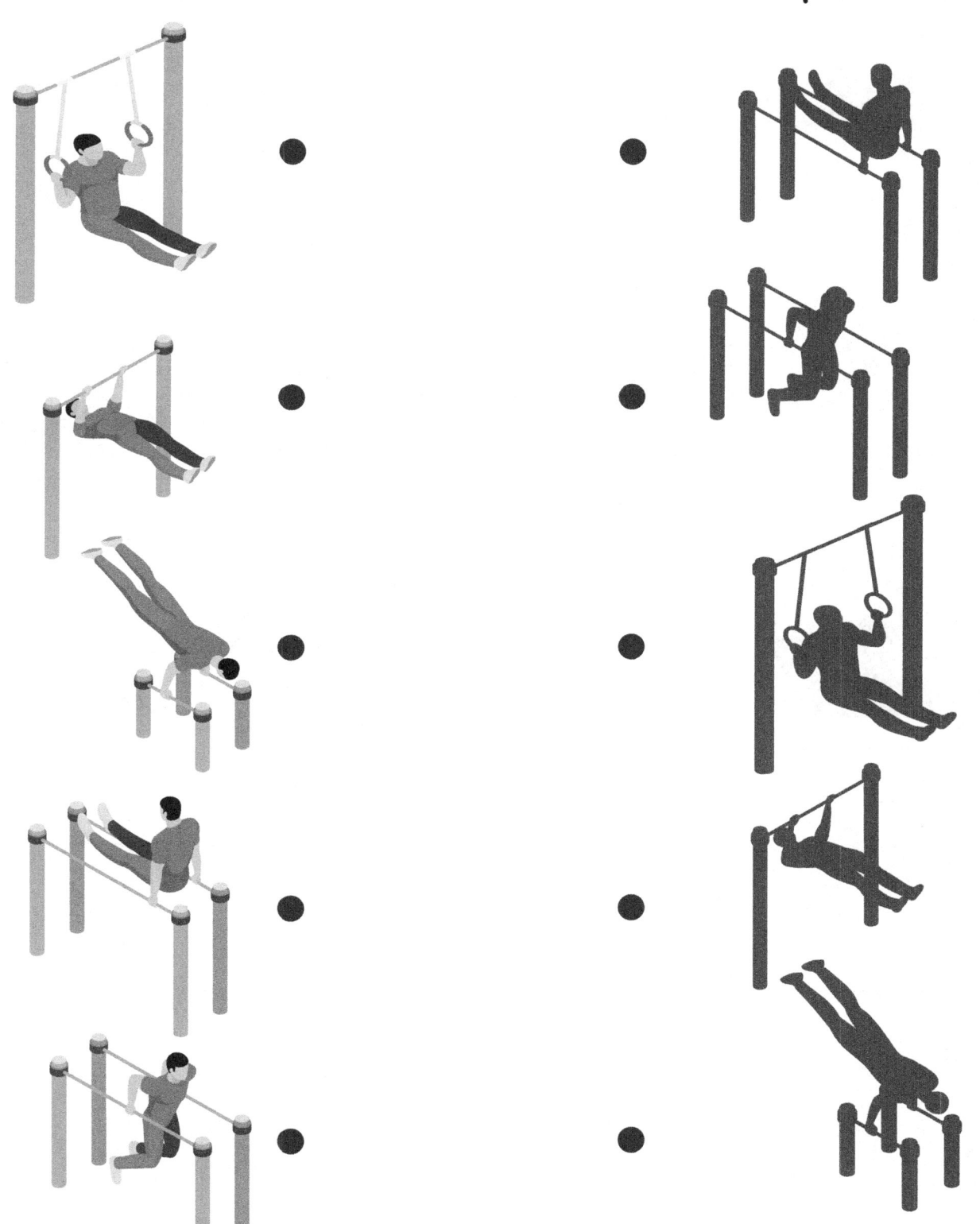

IDENTIFY THE SHADOW

color the circle of the correct shadow

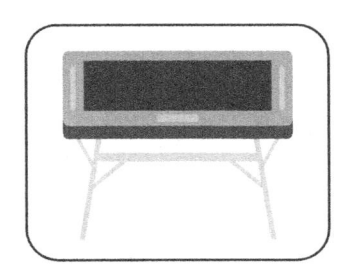

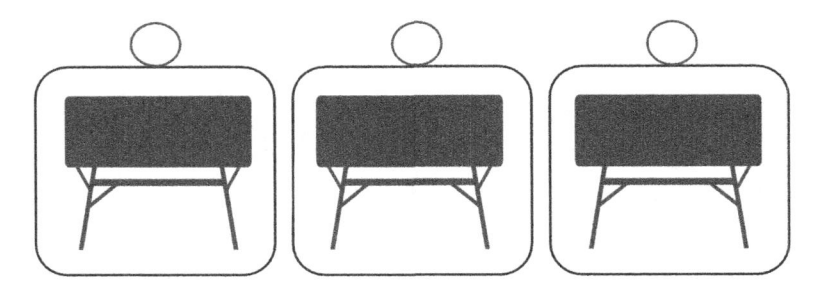

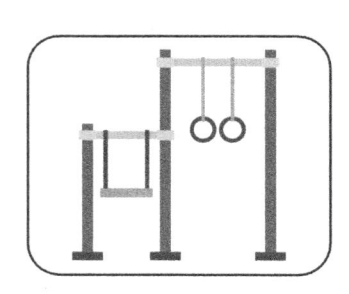

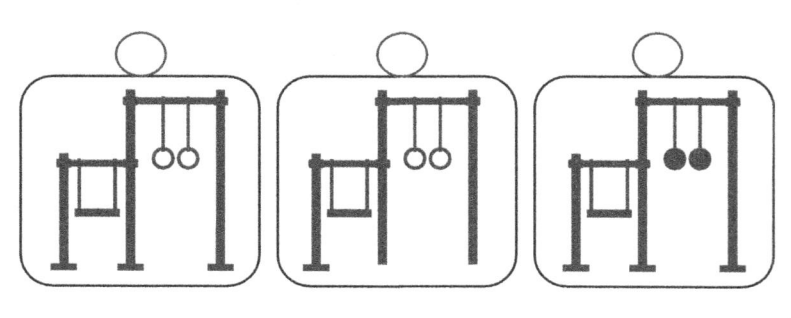

MY GOALS

MY SCHEDULE

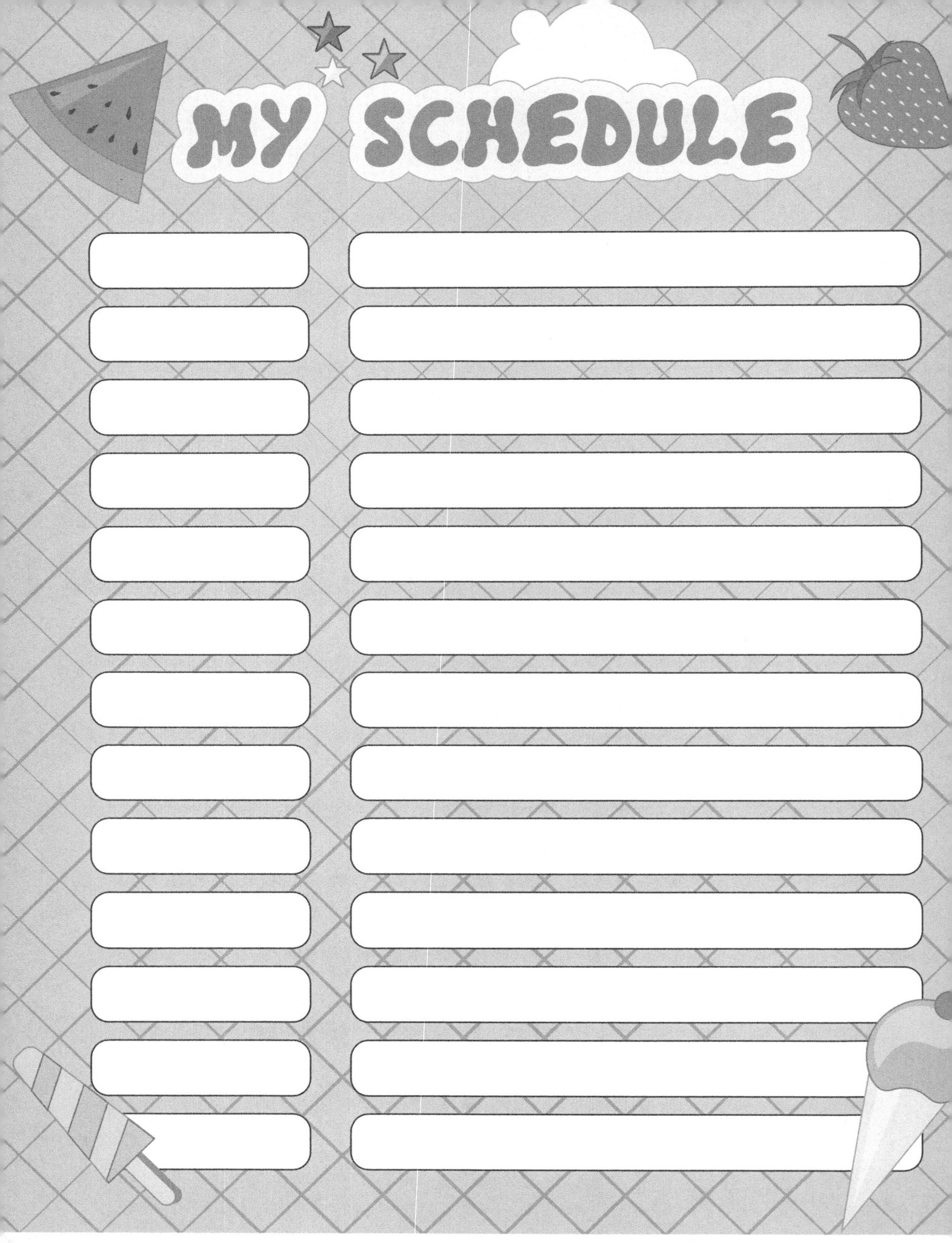

NOTE

WEEKLY PLAN

Saturday
Sunday
Munday

Tuesday

Thursday

Friday
Notes

WEEKLY PLAN

Saturday

Sunday

Munday

Tuesday

Thursday

Friday

Notes

WEEKLY PLAN

Saturday

Sunday

Munday

Tuesday

Thursday

Friday

Notes

WEEKLY PLAN

Saturday

Sunday

Munday

Tuesday

Thursday

Friday

Notes

WEEKLY PLAN

Saturday

Sunday

Munday

Tuesday

Thursday

Friday

Notes

COLORING

Color the picture below

17

WORD SCRAMBLE

Rewrite the correct order of the scrambled words below

lempom heros

_____

litls nirsg

_____

sedalm

_____

taulv

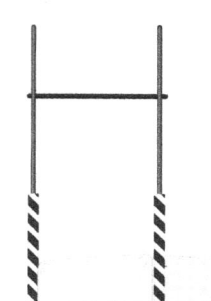

_____

gihh arb

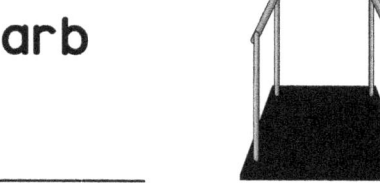

_____

lelpalra sarb

_____

MY GOALS

MY SCHEDULE

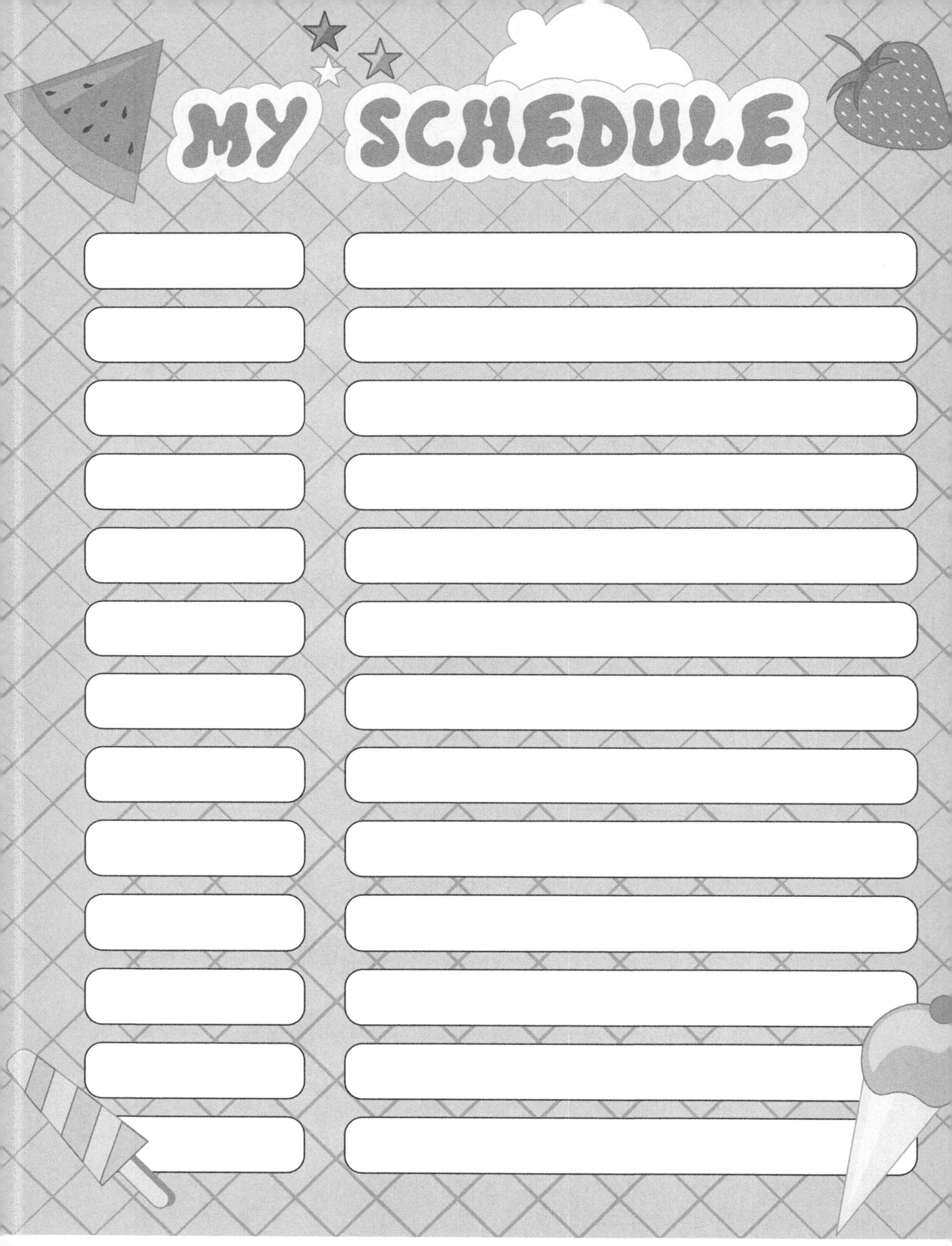

NOTE

WEEKLY PLAN

Saturday

Sunday

Munday

Tuesday

Thursday

Friday

Notes

WEEKLY PLAN

Saturday

Sunday

Munday

Tuesday

Thursday

Friday

Notes

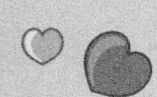

WEEKLY PLAN

Saturday

Sunday

Munday

Tuesday

Thursday

Friday

Notes

WEEKLY PLAN

Saturday

Sunday

Munday

Tuesday

Thursday

Friday

Notes

WEEKLY PLAN

Saturday

Sunday

Munday

Tuesday

Thursday

Friday

Notes

ANSWER KEY

page 9

(A, 1) (B, 2)

(C, 1) (A, 3)

page 10

(A, 1) (C, 3)

(B, 2) (C, 1)

page 11

page 12

ANSWER KEY

page 13

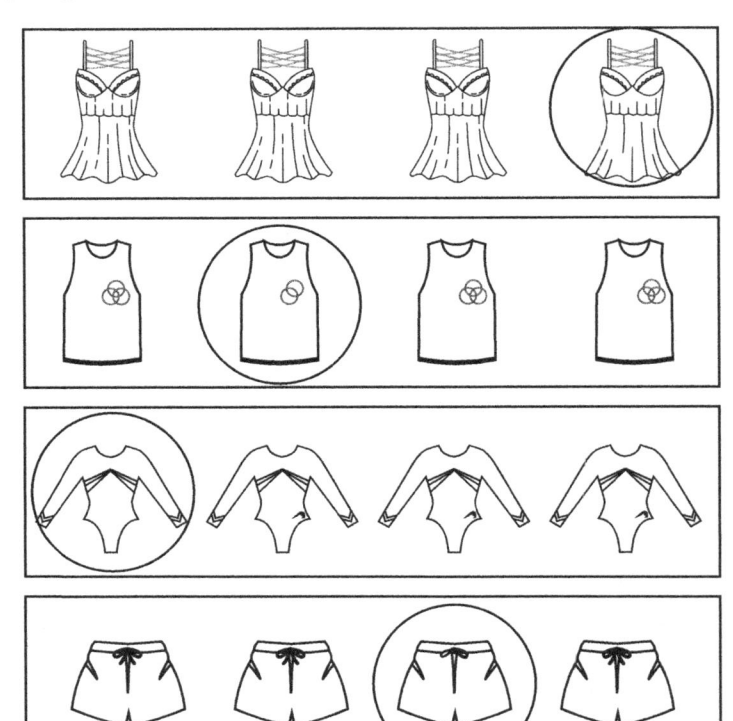

page 14

page 18

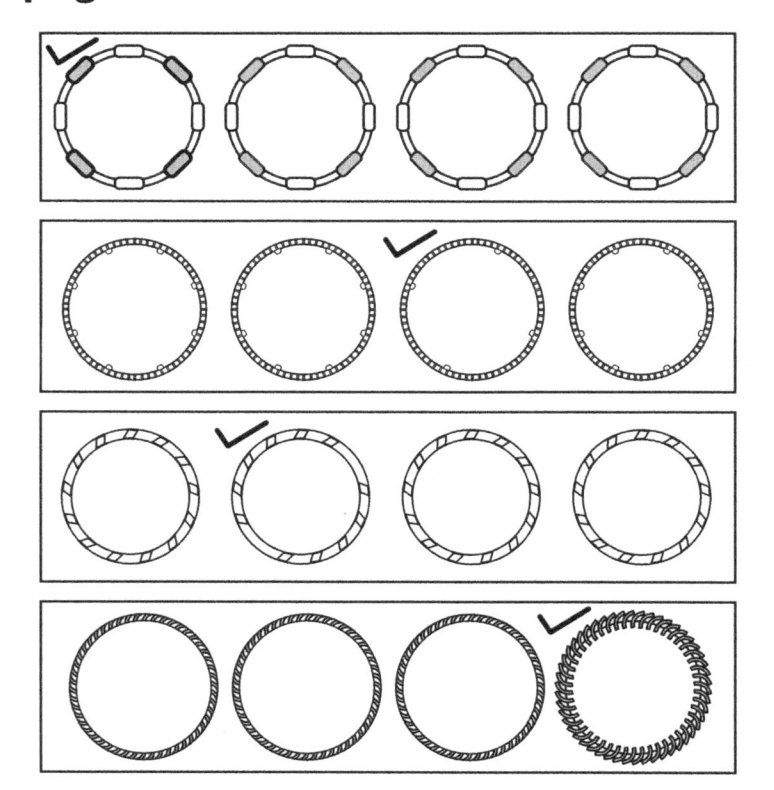

page 19

33

ANSWER KEY

page 20

Word search with: POMMEL HORSE, BEAM, TUMBLING, GYMNASTICS, TRAMPOLINE, BARS, RHYTHM, VAULT, MATS, AEROBIC

page 21

$3 + 2 = 5$

$8 + 4 = 12$

$5 + 3 = 8$

$1 + 6 = 7$

$2 + 2 = 4$

page 23

$5 - 4 = 1$

$4 - 2 = 2$

$4 - 1 = 3$

$7 - 2 = 5$

$5 - 4 = 1$

page 22

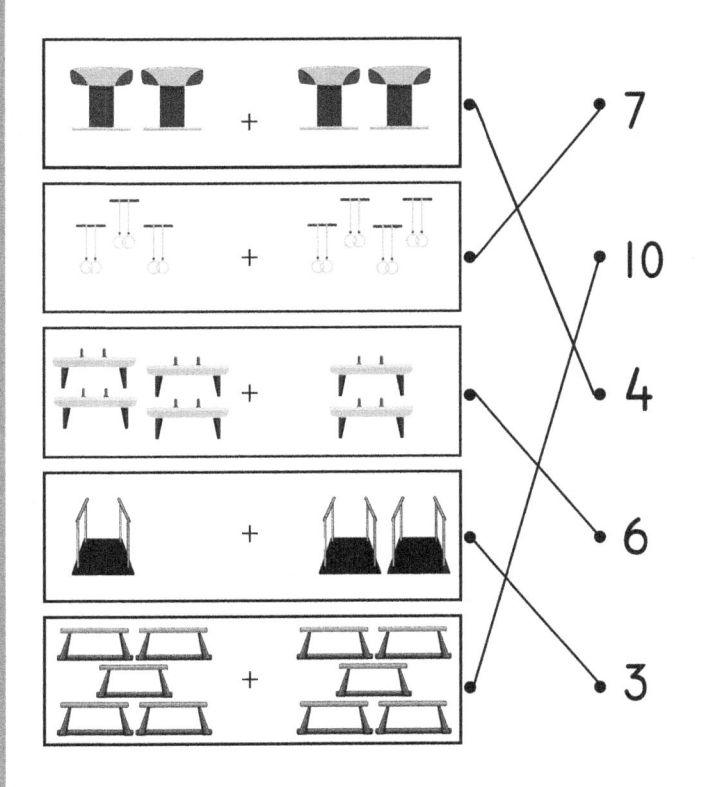

- 7
- 10
- 4
- 6
- 3

page 24

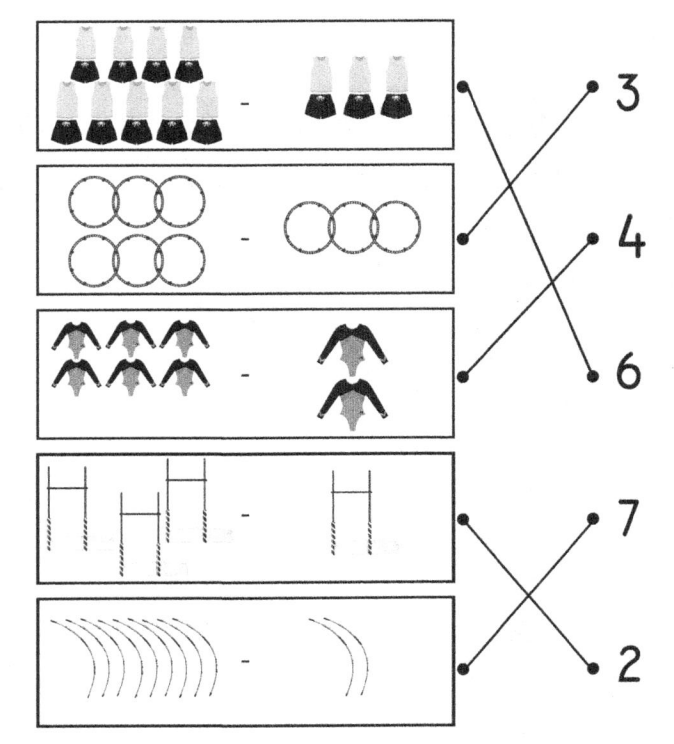

- 3
- 4
- 6
- 7
- 2

34

ANSWER KEY

page 25

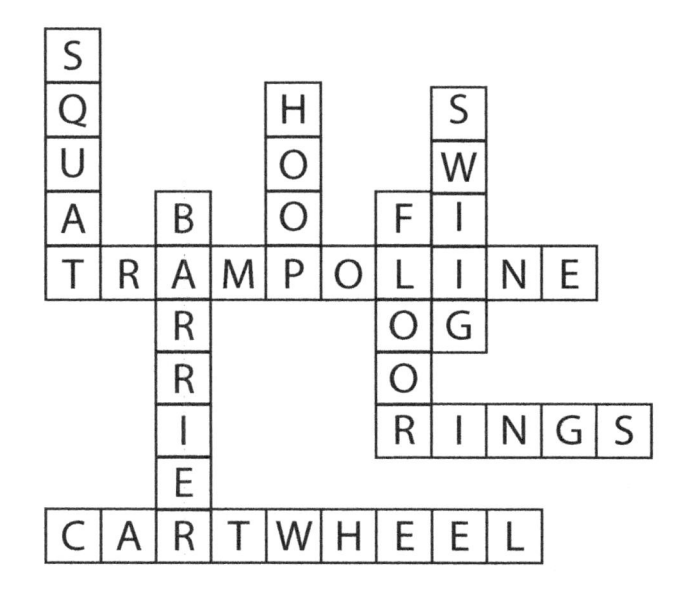

Crossword:
- SQUAT
- HOOP
- SWING
- BARRIER
- TRAMPOLINE
- FLOOR
- LOG
- RINGS
- CARTWHEEL

page 26

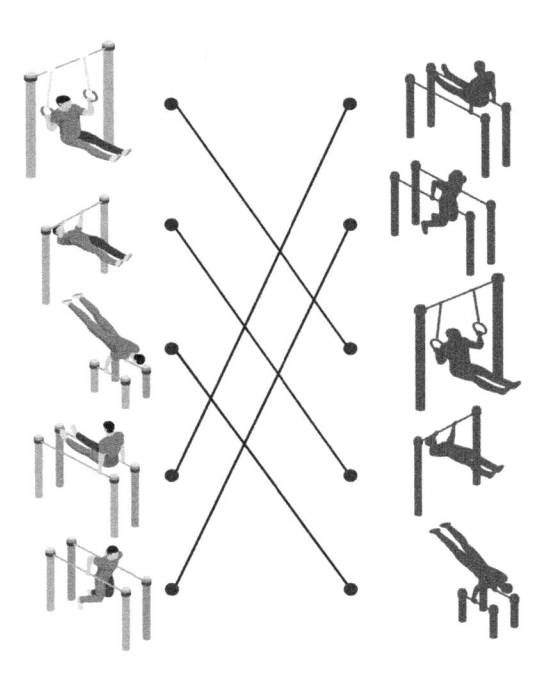

(matching activity)

page 27

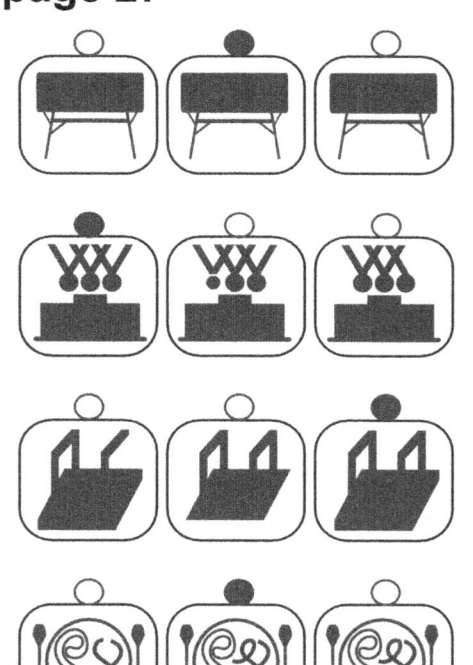

(spot-the-difference illustrations)

page 28

balance
strength
flexibility
swiftness
coordination
endurance

page 29

6	1
9	7
2	11
5	14
13	3

she flipped

page 30

pommel horse   still rings
medals   vault
high bar   parallel bars

35

Made in the USA
Coppell, TX
29 January 2023